T0047110

CULTURE SMART!

BOTSWANA

THE ESSENTIAL GUIDE TO
CUSTOMS & CULTURE

MIKE MAIN

KUPERARD

"The real voyage of discovery consists not in seeking new landscapes, but in having new eyes."

Adapted from Marcel Proust, *Remembrance of Things Past.*

ISBN 978 1 78702 256 0

British Library Cataloguing in Publication Data
A CIP catalogue entry for this book is available
from the British Library

First published in Great Britain
by Kuperard, an imprint of Bravo Ltd
59 Hutton Grove, London N12 8DS
Tel: +44 (0) 20 8446 2440
www.culturesmart.co.uk
Inquiries: publicity@kuperard.co.uk

Design Bobby Birchall
Printed in Turkey by Elma Basım

The Culture Smart! series is continuing to expand.
All Culture Smart! guides are available as e-books, and many
as audio books. For further information and latest titles visit
www.culturesmart.co.uk

ABOUT THE AUTHOR

MIKE MAIN is a businessman and management consultant specializing in leadership, team building, and presentation skills. Born in Devon, England, he has lived in West, East, Central, and Southern Africa for most of his life and is now a citizen of Botswana where he has lived for nearly forty years. In addition to his professional career, he is known as a photographer and a safari guide. He has also written a number of books on Southern Africa and lectured extensively, both regionally and on cruise liners. Although now largely retired, he was a committee member of Transparency International and The Botswana Society, and Chairman of the Maru-a-Pula School Council and the Gaborone Music Society.

COVID-19
The coronavirus pandemic of 2020 affected millions of people around the world, causing unprecedented social and economic disruption. As the impact of this global crisis continues to unfold, in many countries social norms are being challenged, and enduring changes will be reflected in future editions of Culture Smart! titles.

CONTENTS

MAP OF BOTSWANA

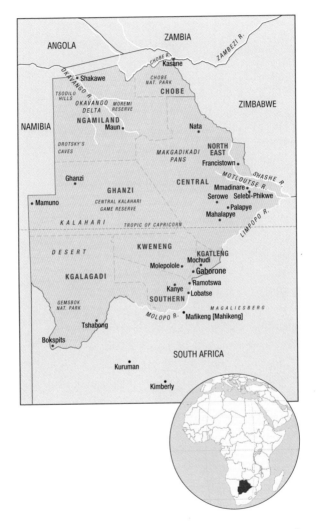

INTRODUCTION

Landlocked Botswana is a country of contrasts.
More than 80 percent is referred to as a desert—the
Kalahari Desert—yet it is not a desert at all. Despite
the endless distances of thorn tree and scrub, the red
sand of the Kalahari contains substantial woodland
and other vegetation, and conceals boundless wealth
in the form of coal, methane, copper, and diamonds:
Botswana is the world's biggest producer of
gemstones.

There are no perennial inland rivers, and no
lakes—yet there is the Okavango Delta, said to be
the largest inland river delta in the world.

In a world where one measure of national wealth
is the time for which a country can afford foreign
imports out of reserves (usually two to three
months), Botswana's time is measured in years.
It is also true that the gap between rich and poor is
growing ever wider, so the visitor will encounter
obvious examples of both wealth and poverty:
expensive cars and big houses, excellent roads and
modern buildings, yet high unemployment and
rural villages with dwellings built traditionally,
of natural materials, without sanitation, electricity,
or water.

Culturally, the people are overwhelmingly Bantu-
speaking, but they are by no means a homogeneous
group, except by classification in the broadest ethnic
terms. In Botswana there are more than twenty

tribes and twenty different, though sometimes related, languages.

At independence in 1966, Botswana was one of the poorest countries in the world; it was also one of the most traditional and conservative. In the years since independence the country and its economy have made extraordinary strides, and Botswana is rightly seen as a model of democratic, planned development. But, for all that, traditional values lie close to the surface, often barely concealed beneath a veneer of modernity. This serves to explain the range of responses and behavior that a visitor might encounter. Many older people are intensely conservative in outlook, while the educated young seem indistinguishable from their peers around the world: enthusiastic, bright, innovative, and utterly modern. All are kindly, welcoming, and, above all, forgiving.

Culture Smart! Botswana introduces you to the lives of the people. It looks at the history that has shaped its society and shows the importance of traditional customs and values. It describes how Batswana live, work, and play, and how to avoid the pitfalls of cultural misunderstanding.

Official Name	The Republic of Botswana	The country is Botswana, the language Setswana, the people Batswana, and an individual a Motswana.
Capital City	Gaborone	
Major Towns	Francistown, Lobatse, Mahalapye, Palapye, Selebi-Phikwe, Ghanzi, Maun, Kasane	
Population	2.3 million	
Area	216,912 square miles (561,800 square km)	
Terrain	Generally flat. Dry desert plateau of woodlands, thorn scub, and grasslands	The Limpopo River lies to the east, the Chobe to the north, and the Okavango forms a vast delta in Botswana.
Altitude	3,281 feet (1000 m)	
Climate	Semi-arid	
Language	Setswana and English	Media languages: English and Setswana
Literacy	96%, in Seswana and English	Adults over the age of 15 who can read and write short simple statements
Religion	Christian, Muslim, ancestral	
Currency	Decimal currency: the pula, with 100 thebe in 1 pula. Approx. 10 pula to the pound sterling and 5 to the US dollar	Credit cards are widely used in towns.

Government	Parliamentary democracy	Parliament consists of 57 elected members, plus 4 specially appointed by the President, the President himself, and the Speaker, making a total of 63 members. Elections are held every five years.
Media	State television and radio, state newspaper, independent newspapers and radio stations	English is the dominant media language.
Electricity	220–230 volts, 50 Hz	Both square and round pronged plugs are used.
DVD/Video	PAL system	
Internet Domain	.bw	
Telephone	Botswana's country code is 267.	Excellent internal and external telephone connections. Two cell phone providers
Time Zone	GMT + 2	
Greeting	A universal greeting, suitable for all times of day or night, is the word "*dumela*" followed by "*rra*" if speaking to a man, or "*mma*" if speaking to a woman.	

CHAPTER ONE

LAND & PEOPLE

GEOGRAPHICAL SNAPSHOT

Botswana is quintessential Africa—vast empty spaces, sparsely populated, often difficult of access, remote, and teeming with wildlife. Most of its 2.3 million inhabitants live on the eastern side and in the northeast with clusters of small towns and villages near the Chobe River and around the Okavango Delta.

With few mountains or hills, Botswana has a fairly uniform topography, at 3,000-odd feet (1,000 m) above sea level. Located in the center of Southern Africa, it dominates the central plateau and, for the most part, is blanketed by varying depths of aeolian sand known as the Kalahari Desert, a remnant of an ancient desert now anchored by a mosaic of vegetation that varies from substantial woodlands

Aerial view of the Okavango River.

through mixed thorn scrub to open grasslands. Fossil dune forms are still visible in parts of the country.

The Limpopo River and its tributaries drain the eastern side of the country, while the Chobe forms the northern boundary. (The word "river" is often used loosely in Africa, and most frequently refers to a sand-filled riverbed without the slightest evidence of water whatsoever. At this latitude, the Limpopo generally has water in it only in the rainy season). The Okavango is a river of considerable size, rising in the highlands of distant Angola, but in Botswana its waters fan out into an immense delta and evaporate or sink into the sand. With the exception of the border rivers and the Okavango there is no open standing water anywhere in the country: there are no lakes, no perennial rivers, and no streams. Evaporation, which is around six feet (just under two meters) a year, exceeds rainfall in every month of the year.

CLIMATE

Botswana straddles the Tropic of Capricorn. It has one rainy season a year that usually starts in November and can last through to March or sometimes April. For the rest of the year, generally speaking, no rain falls. While rainfall diminishes in quantity from northeast to southwest, variability works in the opposite direction. Typically, figures of around 23 to 26 inches (500–600 mm) with a variability of 25 to 30 percent would be recorded for the northeast, while in the southwest they would more likely be 11 or 12 inches (150 mm) with a variability of 80 percent. In the center and south, temperatures can touch or dip below freezing for a few days in winter and in summer can, rarely, top 104°F (40°C). More usually they hover in the upper 90s (30s).

Commonly, the season for visitors is the winter period, with numbers rising from late March, peaking in July/August, and tailing off as temperatures start to rise at the end of September into the grueling months of October and November. This period is favored for its cool temperatures, its endless, blue-sky, cloudless days, and the fact that, with the grass dying off, game is much easier to see. This is a pity, for those who are prepared to risk the heat of summer and the problems of long grass may have the advantage of seeing wildly dramatic thunderstorms, the most stunning cloud formations, and Africa's late afternoon, magical, storm-backed photographic light.

THE PEOPLE

The great majority of the people in Botswana are of Bantu-speaking origin, dominated by Tswana pastoralists who, as one entity or another, have been drifting on to the edges of the Kalahari from the east since the fifth century. As pastoralists, the Batswana are cattle owners first and subsistence farmers second, a situation reinforced by the low or unreliable rainfall. The past was characterized by large traditional villages (of 30,000 or more) with lands allocated nearby and, more distantly, in the undeveloped bush, the "posts" at which people keep their cattle.

Bantu-speaking people were not, however, the first inhabitants: the incoming Bantu found the so-called Bushmen, or San, already in occupation. As happened elsewhere in Africa, these

autochthonous people either moved on, were absorbed, or entered into what has eventually become a subordinate relationship with the newcomers. The San were hunters and gatherers, uniquely adapted to the harsh living conditions of the Kalahari. Today they are in the grip of far-reaching cultural and social change and, as a previously marginalized people, the surviving 60 to 80,000 are struggling for recognition and for a fairer share of national resources.

The Bushman Question

This is a vexed but very topical issue. It is true that the

government is encouraging Bushmen to leave the Central Kalahari Game Reserve (CKGR); and the CKGR was allocated in 1961 for the preservation of game and for Bushmen to follow their traditional way of life. The CKGR is a tough environment and its inhabitants would die without government-subsidized food and water—provided at huge cost. A large village outside the reserve has been built and services provided. The fundamental issue is not about game reserves or diamonds, as some think: it is about political leverage and the ability of a cultural minority (the Bushmen) to garner sufficient influence in any way they can (by a claim to the CKGR, for instance) to protect their own long-term cultural interests.

A BRIEF HISTORY

The Stone Age

Although remains of mankind's earliest ancestors have yet to be found in Botswana, the skull of an eight-year-old child, 2.5 million years old, was found at Taung in South Africa, less than 110 miles (180 km) from the southern border. There is no doubt that Australopithecines also lived in Botswana.

Stone tools lie scattered, and buried, over all of Botswana, evidence of intermittent human occupation over an immense time span. Pebble tools found in the Ngotwane riverbed may be more than a million years old. Certainly, well-formed hand axes found in Gaborone and throughout the country testify to the presence of *Homo erectus* perhaps 500,000 and more years ago.

Middle Stone Age points and scrapers indicate the presence of early *Homo sapiens* throughout Botswana from Lobatse to Maun, from Francistown to Bokspits, and many other places, dating from perhaps 200,000 or more years ago; while Late Stone Age microlithic tools point to ancestral Bushmen just as widely distributed during the last 4,500 years.

Stone Age peoples lived by foraging for food. They collected wild plants, birds' eggs, tortoises, and insects, killed small animals like hares, hyrax, and porcupine, and hunted larger ones like antelope. By 600,000 years ago, and possibly from much earlier, they could communicate and use fire; and from about 200,000 years ago they may have mounted stone points on sticks for use as spears. From about 10,000 years ago they hunted with bows and arrows, made jewelry from ostrich eggshell and bone, and engraved and painted images of animals and designs on rock. These were the ancestors of the modern Bushmen, known in Botswana as *Basarwa*.

The First Farmers
The first Black farming peoples spread west into southeast Botswana in the fifth century CE, bringing with them a sedentary lifestyle, domestic stock, possibly food crops, knowledge of metallurgy and pot-making, and long-distance trade. They lived in settled homesteads, and also collected wild foods and hunted. They must have come into contact with ancestral Bushmen, for the

latter's stone tools are found in farming settlements dating from about the sixth century.

Around 1000 CE, new farming peoples arrived from the east to settle much of eastern Botswana. They built more substantial settlements, sometimes on hilltops, grew crops, raised cattle, sheep, and goats, mined for minerals, worked iron and copper, made pottery, and traded for foreign goods like glass beads and seashells. These were the ancestors of the modern Bakhalagari, some of whose descendants still live in villages in the southeast and also over much of western Botswana.

Ancestral Batswana

It is not known when Batswana (the Tswana people) first entered this country, but dated pottery at places such as Modipe, near Gaborone, suggests they had arrived well before 1600 CE. On the other hand, oral history indicates that during the seventeenth century groups of Bakwena, who had been living along the Marico River in South Africa, began moving westward. With them came the Bangwaketse and the Bangwato, who broke away from them during the eighteenth century after arriving in the country.

When the Batswana arrived in Botswana, they came as small but well-organized groups to settle in areas already occupied by the Bakhalagari. At first, relations were amicable, but soon the Batswana tried

The Batswana's capital "Litakun" (Dithakong) in 1804. Aquatint by Samuel Daniello.

to dominate the Bakhalagari, who moved south and west to get away from them.

The Nineteenth Century

During the nineteenth century there was widespread unrest in southeastern Africa, sparked by factionalism within the Zulu nation, which spread through the tribes of the subcontinent like wildfire. At about the same time the Afrikaners in the Cape Colony, in a movement known as the "Great Trek" (see page 27), started to expand northward. Both these factors caused great disruption in Botswana: new groups, Bakololo and Amandebele, moved aggressively into the area, causing the resident Bakwena and Bangwaketse groups to break up and lose much of their property.

The Bakololo, coming from the borders of Lesotho, attacked the Bakwena and occupied their main village.

At the same time the Amandebele, an offshoot of the Zulus, under Mzilikazi, settled first near Rustenburg and then near Zeerust in South Africa, close to present-day Botswana, raiding that country and demanding tribute of white cattle from the Bangwaketse. Many offshoots of Tswana groups then living in South Africa took shelter with the Bakwena and Bangwaketse.

The Missionaries

During the nineteenth century, Christian missionaries played an important role among the Batswana, a group hitherto almost untouched by European culture and affairs. By 1810, they had visited as far north as Kanye, although the first mission station in Tswana country was established by the London Missionary Society (LMS) near Kuruman in South Africa.

Much has been written about the missionaries, some of it good and some bad. They came from Europe to spread the Gospel and "civilization" in darkest Africa and, conforming to their times, supported both colonialism and capitalism. Even so, they recognized the oneness of humanity, albeit in a paternalistic manner, believing the Gospel would prosper only if the Tswana lifestyle changed, becoming based on good agricultural practices, hard work, and reduced "frivolity."

They deplored polygamy, alcohol, ancestor-worship, and bride wealth (*bogadi*), acquiesced in the inferior status of women, and believed that control of religious affairs had to remain in superior white hands. To establish a suitable framework for a Christian lifestyle they helped foreign traders to establish themselves commercially and spread a modern economy, creating new avenues of wealth for common people; introduced advanced medical practices, education, foreign crops, and eventually a postal service; acted as liaison between the Batswana and the Cape government; helped in the termination of slavery; and advocated the curtailment of Boer expansion into Tswana lands.

The missionary Robert Moffat in 1843. In the background a Tswana chief addresses his parliament.

Although the missionaries recognized the need to keep the Gospel and politics separate, Afrikaner, or "Boer," treatment of the Batswana in the Transvaal eventually forced some of them to take a stand. From 1867 onward, the Reverend John Mackenzie begged Britain to occupy Tswana lands in order to prevent Boer encroachment, and John Smith Moffat, Robert Moffat's son, left missionary service to take a British government post and became involved in the establishment of what was to become Bechuanaland Protectorate and, eventually, Botswana.

Initial efforts to convert the Batswana had little success, but the missionaries were accepted by the chiefs, or *Dikgosi*, for the skills they brought with them and the foreign trade they attracted, particularly in guns and ammunition. To say the missionaries prospered is untrue; by the end of the nineteenth century there were few converts and fewer than ten actual mission stations in Botswana. Their paternalistic attitude upset the new generation of missionary-trained African evangelists, eventually causing some to split away to establish their own churches. Yet the missionaries' impact on the traditional Tswana way of life

Sechele I of the Bakwena was converted by David Livingstone and became an ardent evangelist.

was tremendous. They failed to accept African culture and religion, believing these to be a severe impediment to the Batswana's entering the modern world, yet they recorded in great detail nineteenth-century Tswana life. Some of their records, kept in missionary archives, remain unpublished.

While male missionaries took the lead in all affairs, their wives played an active role teaching reading, writing, homecraft, and the Bible in Sunday schools, visiting Tswana families, and setting an example of friendship and caring for their fellows. Missionary wives probably did more to bring new members to their husbands' congregations, and certainly their female converts became the most successful evangelists among the Batswana. While it was European missionaries who introduced Christianity, it was Tswana evangelists who had the greatest success with their people.

The earliest missionary societies to operate in Botswana, the LMS and the (Lutheran) Hermannsburgs, recognized the need to keep their activities separate and not to impinge upon each other's flocks. The LMS undertook pastoral work among the western Batswana, while the Hermannsburgs established themselves in the east. In Botswana, they were followed by the Dutch Reformed Church, which established itself and built a hospital in Mochudi in the 1870s. Through the years of the Protectorate, they were to be followed by other Churches, such as the Seventh Day Adventists, the

Roman Catholic Church, the United Free Church
of Scotland, and the Anglican Church.

Until 1966 and Independence, and lacking British
financial support, Botswana relied heavily for its
education and health programs on missions and
Churches. It was they who built and staffed the
hospitals in Kanye, Ramotswa, Mochudi, Molepolole,
Maun, and Mmadinare, and schools throughout the
country. Although many Batswana remain animist,
Christianity is the major religion, and many
government as well as all tribal meetings (*kgotla*)
open with a prayer.

The Afrikaners

In 1836, the Afrikaners, descendants of the original
Dutch colonists in the Cape, left that region in large
numbers, crossed the Orange and Vaal Rivers into the
hinterland of Africa, and settled in the lands where
Mzilikazi had defeated the Batswana. After attacking
and driving the Amandebele north, the Afrikaners,
known as "Boers" (Dutch, "farmers"), spread over the
area, forcing some of the remaining Batswana groups
to move westward into the territory of the Bakwena in
modern Botswana.

As the Batswana regrouped in the early 1840s
and tried to reestablish themselves, they seized the
property and lands of the earlier Bakhalagari
inhabitants, forcing them to work and hunt for them,

and they made serfs of the Bushmen, who became their domestic servants and cattle herders, a situation that was to continue until the end of the nineteenth century.

In 1852, Boer settlers living west of Pretoria, in a determined effort to subdue the Batswana, attacked them at Dimawe, southwest of Gaborone. The immediate outcome of the battle was a draw, but the Batswana followed up the attack, raiding eastward, burning Boer homesteads and driving the Boers back to the Magaliesberg mountains, thus permanently preventing the occupation of their land.

The Discovery of Diamonds

The 1860s were to see the discovery of diamonds in Kimberley in the northern Cape and, in 1886, gold on the ridge south of Pretoria, an area that would first be called Johannesburg and is now Gauteng (Setswana, "Place of Gold"). Mining and steady increases in arable farming in South Africa soon attracted Batswana laborers, already long accustomed to traveling over considerable distances to trade their ivory spoons and bangles, copper ornaments, and fur cloaks for sheep and cattle. Now, they offered their labor in the mines for cash wages and on the farms for livestock and grain. Thus, migrant labor in the nineteenth and twentieth centuries became an important part of Tswana life.

Protectorate History

From about 1870, political dissatisfaction and a
shortage of farming land within the South African
Republic (the Boer state north of the Vaal River
that eventually became the Transvaal) led some of
its citizens to attempt the establishment of their own
mini-republics in the area between modern Kuruman
and the Molopo River. They fomented trouble
between different groups of Batswana and took
advantage of this to seize land, eventually establishing
the Republics of Goshen and Stellaland on tribal
territory. Upset by these events and fearing further
strife spreading into modern Botswana, the
missionaries, led by John Mackenzie and John Smith
Moffat, petitioned the British government to take
action.

Bechuanaland, as it was originally called, came
into formal existence in several stages. The first
occurred early in 1884 when John Mackenzie
declared a protectorate over an area south of the
Molopo River (Botswana's present southern border).
This was not initially recognized by the British
government, but in January of the following year the
region proclaimed by Mackenzie did formally come
into "the British sphere" and, at the same time,
administrative jurisdiction was extended northward,
for Whites only, to Latitude 22° South (which
included about the lower third of modern

Portrait of King Khama III, c. 1915.

Botswana). One of the effects of this was to cut in half the lands of the Ngwato people, but, in truth, the declaration had little effect for, as Khama III, who would prove to be one of the truly great Tswana chiefs, pointed out, the northern boundary followed no natural line on the ground so no one knew where it was!

There was not then any intention by Britain to expand her colonial holdings through the Protectorate of Bechuanaland. Indeed, the High Commissioner noted: "Our obligations and interests in Bechuanaland are limited to securing suitable locations for our allies . . . and to keeping open the trade road to the interior of the country." The identities of the "allies" were not stipulated.

By Proclamation No. 1, on September 30, 1885, probably as a result of behind-the-scenes manipulation by Cecil John Rhodes on behalf of his British South Africa Company, the area south of the Molopo shed its protectorate status, and was declared British territory (and thus became a colony). It was named "British Bechuanaland." The area north of the river up to Latitude 22°, formerly only "within the British sphere" was now declared a Protectorate.

For six years, no further changes took place but then, in May 1891, two more steps were taken in the establishment of modern Botswana. British Bechuanaland, the colony to the south of the Molopo, ceased to exist as it was incorporated into the Colony of the Cape of Good Hope.

The Protectorate, that is the portion north of the Molopo and up to Latitude 22°, was extended northward to the Chobe River but excluded the Tati Concession, an area around modern Francistown where gold had been found and over which an exclusive mining concession had been granted by Lobengula, Chief of the Matabele and Mzilikazi's successor, then located at Gubulawayo in southern Zimbabwe (now Bulawayo).

The boundaries of the newly expanded Protectorate were also deliberately vague about the area known as the "Disputed Territory." This was land between the Shashe and Motloutse Rivers that was claimed both by Lobengula and by Khama III. However, on September 27, 1892, both these areas were included in the Protectorate and, in 1899, the final boundary between Bechuanaland and the newly created colony of Rhodesia was decided.

During those early years and right up to 1965, in fact, Bechuanaland was administered from outside its own borders: surely one of the only countries in the world to have an external capital. Initially, the administrative capital was at Vryburg, in the Cape Colony, but on the incorporation of British Bechuanaland into that colony, the capital moved to the town of Mafeking, 22 miles (35 km) south of the Protectorate's borders. (This town, too, has changed its name, and is now correctly known as Mahikeng, "Place of Rocks.")

The modern capital city of Gaborone was built practically from scratch to house the new government that took over the country following Independence on September 30, 1966. At the time of Independence, Botswana was counted among the ten poorest nations on earth. No one then could have predicted the great treasure of diamonds that was to be discovered in the late 1960s and 1970s.

The Late Nineteenth Century

The last decades of the nineteenth century read today like chapters from a novel by Wilbur Smith. In and around Bechuanaland events were taking place that were to have important effects upon the country, in some ways subtle and in some direct. Among the key events are the discovery of diamonds in Kimberley in 1869, of gold around Francistown in 1867, and on the Witwatersrand in South Africa in 1886; the death of Mzilikazi, king of the Amandebele, in Gubulawayo; the increasing number of hunters and traders who traveled extensively in what was to become Rhodesia and who returned with reports of gold and great wealth there; the growing wealth, power, and imperial ambitions of Cecil John Rhodes, prime minister of the Cape Colony; his Pioneer Column and occupation of Mashonaland in 1890; his abortive "Jameson Raid" against the South African Republic in 1896; the Mashona and Matabele uprisings against British rule of the same year; and, also in 1896, the viral disease rinderpest, which swept the subcontinent slaying untold numbers of wildlife, cattle, oxen, sheep, and goats; and the rapid construction of railways.

On a more regional scale the "Scramble for Africa" manifested itself in the southern continent when Germany occupied Angra Pequina (Luderitz in today's Namibia) in 1884, and soon laid claim to what is known today as Namibia. This event alone changed, almost overnight, like the shaking of a kaleidoscope, the perceptions of both Boer and Briton and provided powerful leverage for those with grand visions of empire (whether for personal or national gain).

All of these events, one way or another, had important secondary effects on Botswana. Her minerals, suddenly, were in demand and there was a flood of prospectors, miners, and concession seekers into the Tati area. Tension over rights to the northeast of the country quickly acquired a more visible profile as both Lobengula and Khama laid claim to the so-called "Disputed Territory." The stream of hunters and traders became a river and the eastern side of the country—the only practical route to the north for missionary, miner, colonist, and adventurer—a busy highway for people and goods moving in both directions. Rhodes' machinations created mistrust with the local people and helped destabilize the region: the infamous "Rudd Concession" (a concession to the BSA Company, given by Lobengula, conceding mining rights in what was to become Rhodesia) was little more than a modern con trick. The maneuvering of Rhodes' British South Africa Company and the

The Three Dikgosi Monument, honoring the chiefs who traveled to London to preserve their lands from the encroaching colonists.

activities of other concession seekers who were whittling away at Tswana tribal lands so concerned Khama III and two senior chiefs that in 1895 they journeyed to London to present their case to Queen Victoria. As a result, Botswana remained under the protection of the British Crown.

Over the border in Rhodesia, both the Mashona and the Amandabele reacted quickly, albeit unsuccessfully, against White occupation of their lands. Their rebellions did not stop the "Pioneer" occupation of Rhodesia, however, and served only to multiply the demands upon the ox-powered transportation system. When rinderpest laid the oxen low, Cecil Rhodes' railway from Mafeking to Salisbury took their place, and with the installation of the telegraph there was no stopping the twentieth century from riding roughshod into hitherto largely tribal territories. Change had arrived with a vengeance.

Under a benign British administration the Bechuanaland Protectorate moved slowly into the twentieth century, responding only in the 1960s to Harold Macmillan's "Winds of Change" speech in Cape Town. There was no fight for independence: under the eventual leadership of Seretse (later Sir Seretse) Khama, it came in an orderly, nonviolent, and negotiated manner that delivered the country on to the world stage on September 30, 1966.

Gaborone's skyline.

TOWNS AND CITIES

Botswana's capital is the city of Gaborone, with a
population of some 280,000 or more residents. The
country, since Bechuanaland Protectorate days, had
been administered from outside its borders, and with
the coming of Independence in 1966 it was realized that
there would have to be a capital inside the country. The
small administrative post of "Gaberone's" (a wrongly
spelled reference to Chief Gaborone of the Batlokwa,
near whose principal village it lay) was chosen, and in
the nearby bush and in great haste the new capital arose:
it was only just ready by September 1966. It has seen
phenomenal growth.

Light Humor!

I witnessed the switching on of the first set of traffic lights in 1985 and remember well the large crowd gathered for the ceremony, their applause as the lights changed color, and their still louder applause and enthusiasm when a minor accident occurred within minutes of the formal opening.

Now the city has divided highways, railway flyovers, and many imposing, glass-fronted modern buildings, as well as fifty to sixty traffic lights—or "robots," as they are sometimes known in this part of the world.

The only other city is Francistown, 273 miles (440 km) to the north, with a much smaller population. Other major towns (following the railway up the eastern side of the country) include Lobatse, Mahalapye, Palapye, and Selebi-Phikwe. In the west is the remote ranching town of Ghanzi, and in the north the tourist centers of Maun, at the foot of the Okavango Delta, and Kasane/Kazungula, on the banks of the Chobe River.

GOVERNMENT

The Republic of Botswana is a parliamentary democracy, and elections are held every five years. The Botswana Democratic Party, which, under the leadership of Sir Seretse Khama, won the 1966 elections, has remained in power ever since. There are a number of opposition parties but they are disunited and have not enjoyed great support from the electorate.

There are sixty-five seats in Parliament, fifty-seven of which are elected representatives; an additional six are appointed by the President, who is in turn appointed by the governing party; and seats are reserved for the President and for the Speaker.

While founded on the so-called "Westminster model," Botswana's present system of government comes from a strong and ancient tradition based on

Parliament buildings in Gaborone.

democratic principles. To this day every village has what is called the *kgotla*, a central meeting place usually defined by a high, semicircular enclosure made of tree trunks and located in the shade of a large tree, near the Tribal Offices. Here the chief (*kgosi*) consults his people, here many decisions are made and, above all, it is the place where the people have their say—they are "consulted." It is true that, until fairly recent times, women were not allowed to attend the *kgotla*, and it is also true that it is only superficially "democratic" since, while the people might have had their say, the *kgosi* will still go ahead and do what he thinks is best.

There has been a very small but steady decline in the government's popularity in the years since independence but, at the time of writing, opposition parties hold fewer than twenty of the fifty-seven elected seats The other eight seats, making up the total of sixty-five, are either automatic or appointed by the leader of the winning party.

In recognition of the profoundly traditional nature of the country at the time of independence and of the power and status then held by tribal chiefs, a thirty-five member House of Chiefs was instituted, which continues to this day and serves the government in an advisory capacity. It automatically includes the eight Paramount Chiefs, twenty-two are voted in, and five are appointed by the President.

THE ECONOMY

At Independence in 1966 the new Republic of Botswana was said to be among the ten poorest nations in the world. In eighty-one years of "protection" the British government had sought to raise sufficient funds only to cover the cost of administering Bechuanaland and had invested very little more than was necessary for this purpose. As a result, in 1966 the economy was largely undeveloped. There were no government secondary schools and a total of only some 950 students attending mission secondary schools. Obviously, there was no university, and the handful of graduates had read for their degrees outside the country.

This situation led to a heavy dependence on expatriate expertise that, to a somewhat lesser extent, persists into modern times and manifests itself in occasional outbursts of resentment against foreign workers.

The economy today has its foundations firmly embedded in diamond wealth. There are four diamond mines owned by the government jointly with De Beers in a company known as Debswana. The country is one of the largest diamond producers in the world and the largest producer of gem-quality stones. Debswana is responsible for the running of all the mines and the sorting and marketing, and operates at the very highest levels of professional management. Security is of world standard: there are no "blood diamonds" in Botswana.

The government, wisely, has been trying hard to develop the economy away from an unhealthy dependence on a single commodity. Mining is a big contributor to gross domestic product. Apart from diamonds, copper, nickel matte, and, of more recent date, gold, are equally important. Botswana has vast coal reserves, said to be the second-largest in Africa, that are as yet unexploited, and coal bed methane and solar energy hold the promise of yet another basic energy product.

In pursuit of diversification a great deal of government money has been put into developing the tourist industry. The country is blessed not only with the peerless Okavango Delta but also with huge herds

Elephant swimming. Wildlife tourism is a growing sector of the economy.

of game, and tourism is an obvious development option. Much of the potential exists in Ngamiland District, in the northwest, but strenuous efforts are being made to exploit other parts of Botswana that, although different, have just as many, if not more, attractions.

Cattle ranching received a considerable boost after independence when a contract for 19,000 tons of deboned beef for delivery to the European Union was put in place. The country has never met the full quota but, in the early days, the arrangement was undoubtedly of great benefit. Today one has the sense that the industry is being eclipsed by tourism and other investment opportunities that are more attractive to younger Batswana. Increasingly it is an activity confined to individuals more strongly linked to the traditional past or to a small but growing number interested in professional ranching, with its emphasis on techniques, efficiency, and productivity.

Botswana's credit rating is at a very high level: both Moody's and Standard and Poor's give the country an "A" for foreign currency and an "A+" for local currency.

STATUS AMONG THE FAMILY OF NATIONS

Despite its small size, Botswana is highly respected internationally. It is, of course, a member of the United Nations and subscribes to all standard treaties. It maintains embassies in many countries, including the USA, Sweden, Ethiopia, Japan, Europe, and China, and, as a member of the Commonwealth, has High Commissions in, among others, the UK, South Africa, Namibia, Zambia, and Zimbabwe.

Its small defense force is extremely well-equipped and well-disciplined, and it has played its part in providing troops in Somalia, Lesotho, and Mozambique. Under the leadership of ex-President Sir Ketumile Masire, Botswana facilitated peace negotiations in the Democratic Republic of the Congo. Gaborone houses the headquarters of the Southern African Development Community (SADC).

CHAPTER TWO

VALUES & ATTITUDES

BOTSWANA'S TIME WARP

The Rural/Urban–Rich/Poor Divide

It is essential for any visitor to Botswana to understand how very much more difficult it is to generalize about this country than it is others. Botswana is only fifty-five years from nationwide poverty and a practically non-existent economy, from inadequate education and an almost universal adherence to an intensely traditional, conservative, tribal way of life. In that short space of time the economy has expanded: cell phones, the Internet, corporate governance, big houses, expensive cars, and consumerism have become part of life—for some but not for all.

The young who have had the chance of a good education at college level and overseas experience

are indistinguishable from their kind all over the world: for the most part bright, energetic, motivated, determined. But there are those at the opposite extreme: the elderly who have remained in their villages and whose way of life has remained largely unaltered down the years. And in between are those who are manifestly part of modern life but who hanker after the old ways, and those in the same group who wish to appear worldly wise and sophisticated, yet who are not, and fear above all the possibility of being found out.

The situation carries another layer of complexity in the huge disparity between "haves" and "have nots," the rich and the poor. The nouveaux riches have quickly acquired all the attributes of indulgent, excessive consumerism, and it is not hard to see the first signs of obesity in them and their children. At the same time, the traditional values of intra- and inter-family support are coming under increasing strain, being sacrificed on the altar of "more and better."

Living in Botswana, in any place, at any time, you will encounter anything from the nineteenth century to the twenty-first, and it behoves the visitor to stick to some fundamental rules, and to be patient, observant, and, especially, sensitive.

RECOGNITION

The need for recognition is paramount among the Batswana, and this is true whether one is dealing with junior staff, supervisors, or managers. There is no more powerful piece of knowledge to possess than the fact that recognition is almost desperately sought and, when supplied, wins smiles and greater cooperation and effort. What form does recognition need to take? Anything: from a simple greeting through to thanks, a compliment, praise,

Acknowledging others is basic good manners.

acknowledgment of achievement, congratulations, and so on. Its antithesis is to ignore people, and this will not be well received at all. To ignore even a greeting is considered rude and offensive.

RESPECT

Respect, the handmaiden of recognition, is important to show. It takes the form of "seeing" people, recognizing their presence, never missing a chance to greet individuals, giving others a chance to say their piece (no matter how many times it has already been said), and exercising high levels of patience. Age and seniority are of considerable importance in Tswana life. Older members of a family expect and usually obtain great respect from their juniors. Children are taught to honor and obey their parents and seniors without hesitation or question and to submit to their authority, under the threat of penalty if need be. Older brothers always take precedence over younger brothers, whose services they can freely command.

FAIRNESS AND JEALOUSY

The working and social environment in this country is highly competitive. The economy is growing rapidly, there is a severe shortage of technical and management skills, and many find themselves in positions that are at the limit of, or above, their skill and competency level. For personal and financial reasons such positions will be jealously guarded and every possible competitor will be eyed with suspicion. Office politics can be lethal and staff routinely use words like "revenge," "battles," "jealousies," and mention the need for "fairness." Understandably enough, self-esteem is often low, and it is this that foreigners must manage carefully.

Fairness is often linked to "due process," and many of the more modern Batswana managers stick rigidly to "process," often as a protective mechanism ("If I make sure I stick to procedure, I can't go wrong and can't be criticized").

No Thank You Letters!

I recently presided over a meeting with a number of somewhat elevated individuals attending. One person reported on the impending departure of three members of staff and mentioned the fine contribution they had made. I at once offered to write a "thank you—well done" note on behalf of the group, but was shot down in flames because it would not be "fair." What, it was argued, would other members of staff feel if they left in the future and did not get a letter? Better say nothing to anybody!

ATTITUDES TOWARD OTHER AFRICANS

Botswana suffers from the misfortune of being an oasis of peace, tranquillity, and stability in an otherwise turbulent region. Add in its considerable (relative) wealth, and one has a powerful magnet that lures in the unemployed, vagrants, refugees, the ambitious, every shape and form of individual from abroad, all seeking to benefit from Botswana's success. Local people consider these foreigners a threat: they are seen to be taking jobs from locals and because of this are often resented and sometimes exploited. Because of their circumstances, foreign workers—who are often very hardworking, motivated, and reliable—are extremely vulnerable to any threat that might affect their right to be in the country and to work.

Apart from the fact that foreign workers are seen as taking jobs from locals, it is also true that some expatriate staff—especially those with high-level specialist skills—are resented because of their earning power. The simple truth is that to employ a world-class consultant of one form or another from any First World country it is necessary to pay a First World salary. When these salaries are converted into local currency and the standard perquisites of the job are added in, such individuals will be seen as being extremely well paid, indeed, by local standards, as excessively paid, and as "ripping off" the country. Resentment follows. This aspect of foreign employment is not as bad now as it once was because senior local salaries have climbed, but the problem does make the newspapers from time to time.

Paradoxically, Botswana has many hundreds of students overseas, especially in Australia, the United Kingdom, and the United States, all taking further studies. Equally, a large number work outside Botswana, especially in South Africa. It is interesting to note the reactions of some visiting Africans to Botswana. People from Kenya and Rwanda, for example, are shocked by what they see as the sloth and inefficiency of services here.

PRIDE AND PREJUDICE

Most Batswana have not traveled outside the country;
therefore, for the majority, there is simply no awareness
of how lucky they are compared to elsewhere in Africa,
by almost any measure one can think of. A consequence
of this is that there is not a widespread sense of national
pride. It is certainly beginning to appear, but it is not
an attitude that immediately strikes one.

At the same time, there is definitely a sense of tribal
pride, especially among the more traditional citizenry.
It is easily possible to place the major tribes of
Botswana in a pecking order, ranked from top to
bottom, and in rural areas in particular this pecking
order has a considerable impact upon employment
and social opportunities.

PATIENCE

The Batswana are an extraordinarily patient and
forgiving people. These are a people who have a
tradition of survival in unusually harsh conditions.
Wealth is a new phenomenon but, both now and in
the past, devastating drought is not uncommon,
unpredictable rains are the order of the day, crop failure
is likely, and violent clashes with aggressive outsiders are
not so far removed in time as to have been forgotten.

These circumstances have shaped them and bred a form of stoicism. Even today, because so many things do not happen as they are expected to, people are amazingly accepting, and little objection is raised by the unexpected or by delays.

Standing in Line

This happens a lot in Botswana—in banks, post offices, and government offices. The systems used elsewhere, with numbered tags and flashing signs, are only just beginning to appear and so people form lines. The line is generally respected, but people do cut in. Women are more inclined to take a chance than men. Typically, the Batswana kindly assume that there must be some good reason for it, and say nothing.

CONFORMITY

Conformity is a traditional inheritance. When the grip on life and survival was tenuous, one did not rock the boat. People did not argue with the chief; they did what they were told. People all agreed, conformed: "tall poppies," those who stood out and tried to do or be something different, were not encouraged. Today the Batswana want to appear in the "right" clothes, with the "right" kind of car—and with a cell phone, of course! Naturally, this is changing, and innovation and creative ideas and people are emerging, but they do so against considerable resistance. Such changes are led almost exclusively by the young, talented, and better educated.

AVOIDANCE OF CONFRONTATION

Experience shows that, despite the country's successes, planning and organization is an area of weakness. This is encountered both in the public and private sectors, but more particularly in the latter, where individual responsibilities are invariably greater. There is a widespread lack of effective supervisory skills at all levels. This feeds into an unwillingness to confront, to demand compliance, to insist on specific performance in accordance with agreed standards and deadlines.

The avoidance of conflict is a singularly marked trait among the Batswana: one of their charms is that they are not a confrontational, aggressive people and will generally go to considerable lengths to deal with matters calmly and peacefully. The consequences of this are evident in every aspect of society: for example, the laws on traffic lights, drunk driving, and speeding are poorly enforced partly because it involves confronting and prosecuting others. A long tradition of conformity works against the exercise of initiative and the taking of personal responsibility in affairs outside their private lives.

WORK ETHIC

It is probably true to say of the majority of Batswana that their attitude toward work is shaped by the recent traditional past. For example, it is much preferred that starting times accord with individual preference rather than be fixed at predetermined hours of the day. The view is that time should be a comfort, a convenience, not a master. Arriving late is a common problem.

The so-called Protestant work ethic is not generally part of people's lives. Work is something one has to do, for which one gets paid. For most Batswana it is an experience in which one is directed, told what to do—it is not one in which initiative is seen to have any role. Obviously, there are many exceptions, and modern ideas are becoming more and more widespread, but among the mass of workers such ideas have yet to take hold on a wide scale. There is a tendency for employees to lie low and play small in the modern work context, in which they may feel insecure, thus making it too easy for managers and supervisors to fall into the trap of a "master–servant" relationship.

It is not uncommon to hear, from Batswana themselves, "We Batswana are lazy," but it is important not to misunderstand this statement. As we have seen, the country is changing from an agricultural into a modern, industrial society, and at this point in the process many of the old rhythms still persist. While there may seem at first sight to be some truth in the statement, Batswana can work as hard as anyone else when they wish to do so.

It is probably true to say that the vast majority of people work purely for the money, not for satisfaction or because of what they can bring to the job. Of course there are many, both young and old, who are actively seeking to develop themselves and their talents, who are self-motivated, who are committed to their work, and who aspire to achieve, not only for themselves but for their employers. However, there are very many more who might claim to identify with these goals but who, when all is said and done, will readily move to another job for a little more money every month.

The need to attend funerals has become a great excuse not to be at work, and it is extremely unwise to attempt to conduct business on a Friday afternoon with anyone, government or private sector, who has sufficient authority to be "out"—because they will be!

"BOTSWANA TIME"

Appointment keeping is not Botswana's top-scoring characteristic! Appointments are routinely forgotten or ignored, and it is advisable to phone the day before to confirm, and to phone again an hour or so before any appointment. Equally, timekeeping and punctuality is another problem area. The phrase "Botswana time" accurately reflects prevailing attitudes toward punctuality. At the same time, however, and perhaps driven by necessity, the Batswana have an extraordinary facility for successful improvisation so that lateness or delayed delivery can often be made up for in surprisingly inventive and creative ways.

THE IMPORTANCE OF THE GROUP

There are more than twenty different tribes in Botswana, but tribalism is not an issue. It is the policy of the government and the various *Dikgosi* to play down tribal differences and make more of a national identity. People, however, can tell at once from language or dialect to which group a person belongs, and will know where they stand in relation to one another in terms of the unspoken but widely recognized social hierarchy.

Family remains the basic unit of social organization and in Botswana is inclusive and very extended. With the rapid growth of cities and towns and the urban drift that accompanies it, however, families that traditionally were concentrated in a particular location are now far more geographically widespread than before, and this places destructive strains on family connectedness. Moreover, because of HIV/AIDS and the growing number of parentless dependants it produces, even greater demands are being made upon the extended family system, which is itself changing and becoming ever less able to cope with such additional burdens.

MARRIAGE, SEXUALITY, AND HAVING CHILDREN

It is the aim of every young girl to be married and have children: there is great pride in mothering a child and rearing it. There is a considerable problem today with teenage pregnancies and with single-parent (mother) families. It is said that, before independence, it was very

Young single mother and child in a rural village.

rare for young girls to have children out of marriage. Today it is a common occurrence and there has been much discussion as to its cause. Some point to poor or inadequate sex education at schools, which causes young people to experiment and leads to pregnancy. Others point out that young girls are having children at the same age today as was common four or five decades ago, and suggest that it is not sexual behavior that has changed but that the age of marriage has been delayed. It is also true that, traditionally, it was never the mother, but the aunt, who spoke to a girl about sex: with the depredations of HIV/AIDS and the widespread distribution of families, it is much more difficult for this to happen today with, once again, ignorance leading to unwanted pregnancies.

As in the past, there is some stigma attached to being a single mother, but there are also other difficulties: extracting financial support from the father can be a problem. Although there are laws requiring this, they are not well enforced. Many girls receive no support at all and a child becomes dependent on its mother's larger extended family.

Family size has diminished in recent years. Typically, a woman now in her forties would have been one of six to ten children. Today in rural areas families still tend to be large, but in towns young, educated women are thinking of having only two or three children.

GENDER EQUALITY

This is, as yet, an unresolved social issue. Traditionally, and perhaps superficially, men were on top and women second-class citizens. Women were not, however, completely powerless. Behind the scenes they were always able to exercise some influence, however subtle and covert. As a modern nation, seeking acceptance in a modern world, Botswana has embraced international standards, including gender equality. At government level commendable strides have been made: there are female ministers, female MPs, and women heading influential parastatal organizations (government-owned commercial entities) such as as Botswana Tourism and the Botswana Investment and Trade Centre (BITC), an import and export development agency. Even at local government level the same changes are apparent: there are now two female *kgosi*, for example.

The greatest resistance is encountered at the individual level. Especially among more traditional citizens and among the less well educated, the ideal of male dominance strongly prevails. As women want to feel more liberated and empowered, so such men feel more threatened and often become aggressive. Male on female domestic violence is an issue. The view that women are chattels and sex objects is widespread and partly explains the extensiveness of the HIV/AIDS pandemic in this country.

This situation leads to two interesting paradoxes: all Batswana, of both genders, want to be seen to be treated equally (see Recognition, above) and yet a huge percentage of men will not recognize women as equals. At the same time, if you want something done well (and this is a generalization), a woman can very often be a better bet than a man.

ATTITUDES TOWARD WOMEN

Attitudes are changing, but old habits die slowly. Many older men still look on women as possessions, and versions of that view, diluted in different ways, are widespread. At one extreme, women have few rights and must do as they are told: men have priority. There is greater egalitarianism among the youth of today, and young women are much more confident, self-assured, and assertive. But only relatively recently have women been allowed to sit in the village *kgotla*, and it is not at all uncommon, especially in rural areas, to find that a young woman to whom you are talking is avoiding your eye, having been brought up in the belief that it is disrespectful to look directly at a man.

Despite this, there is no doubt whatsoever that the status of women in society is changing. Women are being empowered, and many are taking charge of their own destinies. As always, it is the young who tend to lead as they adopt the norms of their generation, which, in this age of international communication— through magazines, television, and the Internet—is less

Motswana businesswoman, Gaborone.

constrained by traditional values. To its enormous credit, the government has set an outstanding example in expanding the role of women. As we have seen, there are women in very responsible positions, and others are making their mark in different areas at all levels. There is an ever-growing number of women's groups and the exhortation "*Emang basadi*" ("Stand up, women") is frequently heard.

STATUS SYMBOLS

Rising wealth and growing economic power have led to burgeoning consumerism in Botswana. Compared to pre-independence days, when poverty was widespread and endemic, the Batswana now live in times of relative wealth and it is perfectly understandable that they should be, at this particular stage in the country's development, scrambling for social ascendancy. Outward signs of success assume disproportionate importance: thus elegant houses, laptop computers, smartphones, classy cars, smart dressing, and good grooming all fit the "visible success" agenda very well. A foreigner's personal appearance will be noticed and assessed, and even assistants in a clothing store will look askance at a T-shirt-and-shorts clad visitor, wondering how they can go about in public dressed in that way.

RACIAL ATTITUDES

Feelings of racial superiority certainly exist in
Botswana, although often concealed beneath a thin
veneer. On the other hand, Botswana was the neighbor
of Rhodesia (now Zimbabwe) and South Africa, where
tens of thousands of its citizens worked. Batswana
know from experience what racism feels like. During
the South African liberation struggle military forces
from that country made a number of bloody raids into
Botswana and added to the opprobrium, or at least
suspicion, with which white South Africans in general
and Afrikaners in particular are regarded.

At the same time, conscious of their country's
relative wealth and fearful that it might, in some way,
be taken away from them, the Batswana exhibit a
general sense of xenophobia, strongly influenced by
thousands of would-be immigrants from neighboring
African states seeking refuge and a chance to earn a
living here. Add to this the importation of
expatriates, mainly from Africa, India, and Europe,
who, while vitally necessary because of local skills
shortages, are seen as "taking jobs away from locals,"
and one has a situation where tensions can run high
and resentment is often vocal. Finally there is the fact
that the many tribal groups in Botswana are fitted, as
steps on a ladder, to a well-defined social hierarchy,
which, although never publicized, is well known to

everybody and determines, to a considerable extent, life opportunities: the higher you are on the ladder the better the chances you will get. The Bushmen/San are without doubt on the bottom rung.

In the circumstances it is hardly surprising therefore that, whether one calls it racism, prejudice, or xenophobia, different groups are "ranked" one against another. Generally speaking, South African Blacks are welcomed and regarded as equals, but Blacks from elsewhere are definitely looked down upon, exploited where possible, and labeled "*mokwerekwere*" (outsider). Indians, who play a significant role in the retail and manufacturing sectors, are generally tolerated, but also often resented for their success and for their close-knit and private communities. Whites are generally seen as intimidating, in that they are inclined to speak their minds and make a fuss if something is not done, or not done properly, and, of course, like all expatriates, they are seen as taking jobs.

Paradoxically, perhaps, visitors are welcomed. The Batswana are basically a warm and friendly group, but experience has taught them to contextualize their response. When a visitor is recognized as such, he or she need have nothing to fear and should expect nothing but friendliness.

CHAPTER THREE

CUSTOMS & TRADITIONS

THE CYCLE OF TRADITIONAL LIFE

In ancient times, the Batswana lived in small settlements comprising fairly large families: a man and his wives, with his uncles and younger brothers and their wives, and their children and grandchildren. Such were the Bakwena of Kgabo who, in about 1600 or earlier, broke from their parent group at Rantateng on the Crocodile River in South Africa, moved westward into Botswana, and settled at Dithejwane, near the modern town of Molepolole. They may then have numbered about a hundred to two hundred persons.

The major villages of Botswana (now towns in their own right), Molepolole, Kanye, Mochudi, Maun, and Serowe, for example, may be described as "capitals" of tribally owned land. These capital villages are the homes of the original Tswana parent groups—

Cattle are central to traditional Tswana life, and constitute a form of currency.

Bakwena in Molepolole, Bangwaketse in Kanye, Bakgatla in Mochudi, Batawana in Maun, and Bangwato in Serowe. Many of the lesser villages are homes to foreigners who, historically, placed themselves under a parent group for protection and were given land to establish themselves on within their parent-groups' boundaries. Such villages are numerous and include, around Gaborone for example, Gabane, home to a breakaway group of Balete, Manyana (Bahurutshe), Thamaga and Moshupa (Bakgatla bagaManaana), Mmankgodi (Balete), and Bokaa (Bakaa).

Traditionally, the Batswana moved their capitals frequently, seeking better water, grazing, and, during troubled times, defensive positions. The same is true of the Bangwaketse and others who were constantly on the move during this period. However, since about 1885 there have been no major group movements.

All the villages, large and small, are formed by a number of divisions (*metse*), each comprising aggregates of greater and lesser wards (*makgotla*). The senior division, usually placed fairly centrally and on higher ground, is known as the *kgosing*, or "Place of the Chief," and comprises a number of lesser wards. Other divisions, each comprising a greater or lesser number of wards, surround the *kgosing*. Each division is normally headed by a direct descendant of the founding father of the group. Thus, Molepolole has five divisions, the *kgosing* headed by the *kgosi*, a direct descendant of Kgabo, and four others headed by descendants of Kgabo's sons.

In the past, the *kgosi*, advised by his uncles and in consultation with his people, governed the group and its area, including all the foreigners settled in it. He administered justice, made decisions respecting group affairs, accepted foreign groups, and directed where and under whom they should live. Today, local administration in the villages, and indeed in each tribal area surrounding its capital village, is drastically changed, divided between an elected district council, a land board, and the *kgosi*. The *dikgosi* remain in charge of customary courts and are responsible for certain tribal affairs; but district councils now deal with most local administration, while land boards supervise land allocation.

While these villages were still small, their fields were close by, and the cattle were kept in large herds, moving from one place with a surface water source to another. As villages grew in size, so fields spread farther from them and cattle had to be herded in more distant areas. Families began to have three homes, in the village, at their fields, and at a distant cattle post— the place where their cattle herds were based and watered. When the rains began, women moved to their fields to till and plant, returning only after the harvest, while men and boys looked after the cattle.

To a large extent, the traditional system continues, although some people have settled permanently at their fields and cattle posts. As paid employment increases, many people now work in commerce, industry, and government service, often employing a foreman and herders at their cattle posts, while the elderly remain in the villages looking after children attending school.

The cycle of traditional life is driven by the seasons and, principally, by the advent of the annual rains— crops and food supply are critically dependent upon rainfall. Although rain may sometimes fall in September, typically, plowing of the fields will wait until the "proper" rains fall in October or even November. Men will plow the fields using a single-furrow metal plow drawn by two to four oxen or a team of donkeys. Increasingly, however, either through government financial support or as a commercial transaction, some farmers hire a tractor to do their plowing for them. Aside from a very few large-scale commercial farmers there are some traditional farmers who own their own tractors.

While the soil is still damp, seeds for sorghum, maize, groundnuts, or pumpkins will be planted and protected as far as possible from birds and animals until harvesting in April or May. Looking after the fields and harvesting the crop is the task of women. Often, in the fields, there will be a carefully prepared area where the crop is winnowed before being carried back to the village for storage in special storage bins called *sefalana*. These come in many different shapes and forms, but basically they are made with branches and wooden staves plastered with mud and mounted on large stones to keep them off the ground. Most people make a practice of giving a small part of their crop to the *kgosi* and/or their local church as a token of thanks for the safe gathering of the harvest.

Botswana is not self-sufficient in food production (more than 80 percent of what is consumed in the country is imported). This is partly attributable to the risks involved in dry-land farming. A series of successive droughts are not uncommon and peasant farmers cannot continue to absorb the costs of annual crop failures. Increasingly they turn to the formal economy, seeking paid work, diminishing still further the quantity of food grown in the country.

RAIN SHRINES

Good rains at the right time are obviously critical to the success of any harvest, and so it is not surprising that rain is central to the traditions of all agriculturalists. In Setswana the word "rain" is *pula*, and an indication of the importance of rain is reflected in the fact that all public speeches end with that word called out as an exclamation: "*Pula!*" In Botswana, individuals or tribes (such as the Hambukushu, who live around the panhandle of the Okavango Delta) who are believed to be able to cause rain are regarded with special respect.

Rain shrines are sometimes encountered in the bush. Typically such a shrine will be in an isolated and remote place, in a ravine or a rocky outcrop, for example, and can be easily missed by the casual eye. Usually the wax from four or five candles will be seen in a rough circle on some stones; on a stone in the center of the circle will be shards of broken pottery and a collection of small coins of low denomination. The money represents a gift, and the broken pottery underlines the spiritual link with ancestors whose intercession is being sought to help bring rain. Sometimes on a low, isolated hilltop one may come across a carefully laid bonfire, as much as 4 or 5 feet (about 1.5 meters) high. It may sit there for years awaiting the next time the local inhabitants feel the need to ask their ancestors for assistance in making rain. It will be lit, and the belief is that the rising smoke will take the requests for help to their proper destination.

THE CATTLE POST

As pastoral people, the Batswana hold cattle to be of special importance. Traditionally cattle distribution was controlled entirely by the availability of surface water or

A village *kraal*, or enclosure, where the cattle are kept safe at night.

the presence of hand-dug wells, usually located at the edge of pans. In this way cattle numbers were held in check due to limitation of the water source. Since the 1930s, however, borehole-drilling technology has been available, and with deep boreholes penetrating ancient groundwater, vast tracts of wilderness were opened up for ranching. So it was that cattle posts (the place where a man will drill his borehole, locate his staff, and keep his cattle) have proliferated across the former unoccupied wilderness of the Kalahari. Hand-dug wells were used to find water in suitable places at about 20 to 30 feet (about 7 to 10 m), and early boreholes needed to be drilled from 150 to 450 feet (50 to 150 m).

With water more widely available, cattle numbers rose dramatically and reached such a level that, at independence, the beef industry was seen as the only hope for economic development (diamonds not then having been discovered). In the 1980s, for example, it was widely held that cattle outnumbered people by about four to one!

Today, it is increasingly difficult to find unoccupied areas where groundwater is available. As would-be ranchers are forced ever farther into the Kalahari, it is being found that not only are traveling times and distances from towns getting longer, but the groundwater is much deeper, often more than 1,000 feet (350 m), and drilling the boreholes is very much more expensive.

Today there are government rules about locating new boreholes—each must be more than 5 miles (8 km) and sometimes 9 miles (17 km) from any other borehole—and a prospective rancher will need permission from the local Land Board to use a selected area of land. Then all he has to do is find the money for a borehole; if he is successful in hitting water he has a cattle post, and to this point he will move his cattle.

Cattle posts are not fenced, and the animals range free, sometimes under the eye of a herder (*modisa*, pl. *badisa*), sometimes unattended. There are few places in Botswana today, outside national parks, game reserves, or wildlife management areas, where large predatory mammals offer any significant threat to the encroachment of cattle. *Badisa* are responsible not only for watering the animals every day, or every second day, but also for placing them in a *kraal* at night (depending on which part of the country), maintaining the water pump, monitoring fuel used, and, most importantly of all, accounting for every single animal to the owner when he makes his irregular visits to the cattle post.

Only at long-established or older cattle posts will the owner have built a conventional house. At most places there will only be a traditional hut, or sometimes a caravan. Occasionally owners bring a portable generator with them; otherwise there is no electricity and no running water. The *modisa* will live in huts with his family. Unless he is a member of the owner's family he will almost certainly be from a tribe considered to be very much lower on the social scale. In many parts of the country Bushmen, or San, are employed as *badisa* and will invariably have many of their extended family with them. A 1991 survey showed, in one part of the country, that twenty to forty San on a single cattle post was not uncommon: in one case more than 120 individuals were found, only a few of whom were actually employed and received any remuneration.

Payment in Kind

Payment for employees at cattle posts is not controlled by legislation and is typically very low—probably now between 50 pula and 150 pula (US $5–15) a month—but employees and their families are entitled to free consumption of the milk, and to the flesh of any animals that die. In one survey a Bushman herder, smiling knowingly as he looked at his questioner, said, "You know, it is surprising what happens to a cow when you put a plastic bag over its head!"

The pervasiveness of cattle in the culture explains the importance and popularity of meat, but milk and milk products are equally valued. For example, a staple of the cattle post diet is soured milk, called *madila*. Milk is collected and soured, and the semisolids poured into a salvaged fine-weave sack, which is hung for some days while the whey weeps. The end product is very popular and enjoyed throughout the country. In towns the product is available commercially.

Traditionally, cattle are thought of in the same way as a bank account, and the desire is to have as many animals as possible. It is considered extremely bad form, therefore, to ask a man how many cattle he has: this is akin to asking a man from the West how much he has in the bank. Any reply you get will be hesitant, vague, equivocal, or wrong! If the family needs money, and the man agrees to the expenditure, cows will be sold to raise the necessary cash.

GOATS

Not every Motswana (a person from Botswana) can afford to have cattle, but almost all in the rural areas have goats, which are often referred to as the poor man's cattle. Goat will be eaten much more frequently than beef. Herding goats, as with herding cattle, has

Goatherd on the move in a dry riverbed.

become increasingly difficult to manage as the demands
of the national educational system mop up potential
young herders and take them off to school. Some groups
have solved this problem in a rather ingenious way:
taking puppies from their mother at the earliest possible
moment, the young dogs are raised with goats so that,
by the time the dogs are grown, they appear to think of
themselves as goats. Goats are always corralled at night,
the dogs with them, and on the following morning,
when released to graze, dogs and goats travel as one.
Should one see such a free-ranging group, approach
with caution, for the dogs will be vicious in their
defense of the herd, protecting them during the day
and traveling back with them to the homestead in the
evening.

OTHER ANIMALS

In the rural villages, and in the countryside generally, visitors may well see animals being regarded and treated in a way with which they are unfamiliar, and may well view the experience negatively. Dogs are generally kept for hunting, will accompany their owner into the bush, and will, with luck, help to start, chase, and corner a hare or a small antelope. The dogs will get some of the offal and are otherwise fed on whatever scraps are to be found. Often they simply starve to death, and the sight of these emaciated creatures limping around a village is not easy to bear.

Horses and donkeys are hobbled and left to roam free. Often front legs are tied so closely together that the animal cannot move except by a series of hops, making progress very slow. Some people will wean a calf from its mother by pushing a porcupine quill into the soft flesh of the calf's nose, thereby preventing it from suckling. Values and attitudes are different, and whatever one might feel it is as well to respect those differences.

RELIGION

Thanks largely to the endeavors of the missionaries in the nineteenth century, Botswana today is nominally a Christian country. There is complete religious freedom, and there are many different communities, including Anglican, Roman Catholic, Methodist, Dutch Reformed Church, Lutheran, United Free Church of Scotland, Seventh Day Adventist, Jewish, Muslim, Hindu, Buddhist, and Baha'i. In addition there are many independent African Churches, foremost among which is the ZCC (Zionist Christian Church).

Despite the prevalence of formal religions, animist thinking is pervasive and the practice widespread. Before the advent of Christianity, the Batswana already had the concept of a supreme being whom they called *Modimo*. This entity is seen as all-powerful, all-prevailing, awesome, and thus somewhat remote, distant, and not directly approachable—interestingly, in many ways, not dissimilar to the idea of a "super chief." It is because of the remoteness of this entity that ancestors are seen as being so important, for they play the role of intercessors—messengers who take the pleas and requests of ordinary people to a spirit that controls all destiny.

We have already seen that rain shrines are places in the bush where pleas for rain are made, but evidence for the huge importance of ancestors is everywhere to be seen. The Batlokwa, for example (a Tswana tribe whose tribal lands and capital village abut the city of Gaborone) bury their elderly dead within the courtyard of the family residence and, after the passage of some weeks, will build a hut over the grave. In this way it is sought to keep ancestors closer to the family and to events that shape its well-being: thus they will be in a better position to understand the family's difficulties and will know how best to help find a solution.

Ancestors are never far from the mind of the Motswana: good harvests are acknowledged by a donation to the church and to the chief; occasionally traditional beer will be poured over the trunk of a tree out in the fields or on a corner fence post of a field; where there has been much misfortune in a short period of time a pot containing food might be buried in a field or near the home.

For similar reasons, graves are revered. Among many older people it is believed that if one dreams of a dead person it is necessary to go to that person's grave, remove a pinch of soil from it, and either put the soil into bath water or sprinkle it into drinking water that will be used by the family.

TSWANA TRADITIONS

Part of what makes Botswana such a fascinating country, and the Batswana such interesting people, is the simultaneous and parallel presence of two very different worlds: the old, traditional way of life, and the modern, Western style. The boundaries between these two worlds are often blurred, and sometimes both are evident at the same time. It is possible, for example, for an observer to see a young pregnant Motswana girl walking along the street in the shadow of towering, glass-fronted office blocks, passing between smart expensive cars, aiming for the newly deposited clay on a termite tunnel or a termite mound, and pinching a little of it between her fingers before eating it in the belief that it will clean her womb and strengthen her baby.

Among older people, there are thousands of cautionary or advisory phrases, known in Setswana as *moila*, still in use: visitors would probably recognize them as "taboos." The young are no longer interested, and unrecorded *moila* are rapidly being forgotten, but the older generation will share them with you. They are very much like Western superstitions, and it is easy to believe that they have the same original purpose: to help in the acculturation of the young and to protect people from harm.

For example, one may not go to the hut next door after dark to borrow salt; one may not go to the hut next door after dark to get some fire; a menstruating woman may not walk across a newly planted field; black pots must never be passed behind a person at a fire; pots by the fire must never be touched by the foot, and so on.

It is easy to understand how, in any society, being fat might be taken as a sign of wealth and good health, and it was no less so in Botswana—large buttocks, breasts, and bellies added up to a picture of admired obesity. Today, while young Batswana women strive to keep their slim and shapely figures older generations are still admiring the "woman of traditional build," as Alexander McCall Smith described it. Indeed, so deeply ingrained in the body of tradition is this idea that there is a Setswana word to describe it: *mohumagadi*, referring particularly to the wife of a chief who, ideally and reflecting the wealth and status of her husband, should be fat and therefore healthy.

By far the most widely known or remembered of Tswana traditions are the institutions of *Lobola* (bride wealth), *Bogwera*, and *Bojale*. *Lobola* is discussed at length on page 107. *Bogwera* and *Bojale* are the initiation rites through which young men and women once had to pass in order to attain full adult status. To understand these ceremonies more clearly, it is necessary first to understand the regimental organization of a tribe.

TRIBAL REGIMENTS

In days gone by every Tswana tribe maintained a system of so-called age regiments (*mephato*), and every member of the tribe belonged to one. There were separate regiments for men and women and they were called upon from time to time for services to the tribe as a whole—defense, big public works (such as building schools or small dams), or large-scale hunts being good examples of their former use. A regiment would be formed every few years at the command of the chief, would be led by a royal, and would include all the young men or women who had not yet been initiated and who were usually between the ages of sixteen and twenty years. The number of men in a regiment would depend on the size of the tribe and might include anything from fifty to several hundred individuals. The name given to the regiment would identify its members ever afterward, and it would help to create a strong feeling of unity and solidarity. Regiments were an effective means of binding together members of the tribe in a manner that cut across village, ward, and family ties and engendered tribal unity.

The rules for women's regiments were much less rigid and the requirements much less stringent than for men. Often there was no formal gathering: women simply took on the name of the regiment given to their male age cohort and would not be recognized as belonging to any such regiment until called upon by the Chief to perform some specific task.

Bogwera and *Bojale*

Initiation ceremonies took place for whole regiments at a time. These ceremonies for young people (*Bogwera* for boys and *Bojale* for girls) are, for the most part, no longer part of tribal life in Botswana, although the Bakgatla, who live in Mochudi, a town some twenty-four miles (forty kilometers) north of Gaborone, still claim to undertake the ceremony. (The last known event took place in 1990 and involved 1,200 boys and young men). In one form or another it may also be continued by the Balete and the Batlokwa tribes, both of whom live fairly close to the capital. Early missionaries considered it an evil institution, and did all in their power to suppress it. Progressive chiefs thought that it interfered with the advancement of education and religion, and helped to engineer its demise.

In essence, a male regiment would set up a camp in a remote or secluded place and be away from all villages for as much as three months. Under pain of death participants were forbidden to divulge any of the secrets of the ceremony to women or noninitiates, who were not even allowed to approach the regiment's camp. In the camp, the boys were first circumcised; then, in the days and weeks that followed, they were taught secret songs that exhorted them to honor and obey the Chief and the tribe; to honor, value, and respect cattle and so to look after them carefully; to attend the *Kgotla* regularly and to ensure that its fire never went out; to honor and obey older people; and more. There was also instruction in sex, on the duty to procreate, and on the rights, obligations, and duties of marriage. Isaac Schapera, whose *Handbook of Tswana Law and Custom* was compiled in the 1930s, also records that the young men were subjected to semi-starvation, considerable discomfort, torture, and strenuous hunting expeditions, all with the purpose of hardening them into men.

A man who had not passed through *Bogwera* was not considered a man, whatever his actual age. As such, he would not have been allowed to sit or eat with other men or to take part in tribal discussions; nor would he have been allowed to marry, and he would have been regarded with contempt by the women.

Today, the ceremony of *Bogwera*, where it takes place, is in a much-attenuated form. Hunting, following what game can be found, moving camp from time to time, and understanding through instruction by the elders what is expected of them as men, remains an important part. Circumcision has been completely abandoned, secrecy is no longer stressed and, especially for the modern youth, it is not even considered necessary either to pass through the rites or to belong to a regiment.

Bojale, the women's equivalent ceremony to *Bogwera*, is practiced by only a few tribes today and, compared to the past, is conducted in a much-modified form. Never, however, did it involve female genital mutilation although, long ago, the Bakgatla did mark the passing of this important rite of passage by a small branding on the inner part of the right thigh, close to the vulva. This is no longer done today. Instruction consisted of time spent in the bush being lectured by older women on matters concerning womanhood, domestic and agricultural duties, sex, and behavior toward men. Finally, after a wash in a nearby river, the women might parade before their chief and be given a regimental name.

It is doubtful that any of the modern young women working in the corporate offices of Botswana's big companies would have participated in *Bojale*.

RELIGIOUS AND NATIONAL HOLIDAYS

In many cases, if the date of a holiday falls on a weekend, the following Monday is a holiday.

January 1 and 2 New Year

March/April Good Friday, Easter Saturday, Easter Sunday, and Easter Monday

May/June Ascension Day

May 1 Labor Day

July 1 Sir Seretse Khama Day

July 17 President's Day

September 30 Botswana Day

December 25 Christmas Day

December 26 Boxing Day

CHAPTER FOUR

MAKING FRIENDS

It is difficult, but not impossible, to make friends in Botswana, and there are a number of reasons for this. The cultural divide between foreigners and the people of Africa is very wide. It is perhaps for this reason that it is easier to make friends with those who have lived in the West: the gulf for them is not as wide. Generally speaking, many Batswana find it uncomfortable to attend an unstructured, informal social occasion with foreigners. It takes time to get to know one another, to overcome and understand the differences in culture and language, and often visitors do not have this time. For those staying longer or intending to work in Botswana, the secret is to show respect, be patient, not be judgmental, and, above all, to show interest.

Obviously, the first step toward making a friend is to spend some time in each other's company, and there are various ways to do this. Working in the same office might be one way, or finding a common interest, such as sports, another. Given that sufficient common ground is discovered, there is nothing to prevent the formation of a deep and rewarding friendship. It is as well to recognize, perhaps, that in all societies there are varying levels or depths of friendship, and few people have many really close friends.

Experience in the tourist industry, for example, shows that most promises of friendship with visitors start with an exchange of photographs and end there. In this context the income gap between a visitor and the type of Motswana he or she is likely to meet is so large that there is a risk that the disparity will distort the budding relationship, leaving one side hoping to benefit considerably in material or financial support and making it unclear what the relationship is really about: is it true friendship, or is it taking advantage of somebody who appears to be offering a helping hand?

WORK AND SOCIAL LIFE

As we have seen, work and social life are quite separate, and socializing in the context of a work situation is very limited. In a small business of, say, ten to fifteen employees, there may be a Christmas meal at a restaurant, or perhaps an occasional barbecue (referred

The ubiquitous *braai*.

to in Botswana as a *braai*, after the Afrikaans *braaivleis*, "to cook meat") on the premises. Ordinarily, senior staff will go home for lunch and workers will buy food from a vendor on the street, eating wherever they can find a place to sit. Very large businesses may well have canteens, where there may be some socializing over lunch, although very often such establishments have two dining rooms for different levels of staff—also serving slightly different food.

GREETINGS

It is extremely important on all occasions to greet Batswana, who consider it very rude to ignore others.

The basics are simple: a universal greeting, suitable for all times of day or night, is the word "*dumela*," followed by "*rra*," if speaking to a man, or "*mma*," if speaking to a woman. When greeting any group of two or more (mixed or not), use "*dumelang*," instead of "*dumela*." Handshakes are normal among men and women.

EXPECTATIONS OF OUTSIDERS

Visitors will automatically be seen as wealthy, and therefore the expectation is that you will be generous. This thinking is not strictly traditional in origin, although it has its roots in a past era when chiefs were wealthy and, in times of crises, looked after their people, providing food and protection. Now the tradition is somewhat exploited, and visitors are often accosted in the streets, by children, teenagers, and young adults particularly, with the request to "Give me."

CLUBS AND ASSOCIATIONS

Many Western societies and associations exist in Botswana, and are supported by both citizens and expatriates. They include Rotary, Lions, Ladies Circle, and Freemasons. Overseas membership is readily acknowledged, and new members are always welcome.

Membership of such associations is a good way to make contact with local people and to begin to form a network of associates.

There are sports clubs in both cities and some of the larger towns. These include cricket, rugby, and squash, all supported almost exclusively by expatriates, and tennis and golf, which have much broader support. It is in the golf clubs that much business entertaining takes place and, as with the other clubs, provides the ground where opportunities for forming friendships might well be found.

The Botswana Society is unusual in that it produces an annual journal (*Botswana Notes and Records*) and holds occasional public lectures, outings, and symposia. Membership is inexpensive, and the Society's members are a mine of information about the country and its people. The Kalahari Conservation Society, which has a focus on matters environmental, also hosts occasional public lectures.

INVITATIONS HOME

It is not the habit, generally speaking, for Batswana to invite people to their homes other than for big occasions like weddings or christenings. Nor is it the norm to "entertain" in the same way as people from the West, for example, might do. Rather, the Motswana issues no invitation at all but expects that, if you wish to visit, you will do so at a time and on a day of your choosing, without prior arrangement. One "pops in," as they say, and takes a chance on their being at home. Invitations to dinner will usually come exclusively from the expatriate community.

GIFT GIVING

Corporate companies sometimes give gifts such as a bottle of whiskey at Christmas, and there is no doubt that a small bar of chocolate or one or two sweets does wonders toward improving service at the opposite end of the scale! It is the gesture of goodwill, the thought behind it, rather than the item itself that is important. However, by and large, the giving of gifts as a means of facilitating business is not followed.

If you are invited to dinner it is customary to take a bottle of wine for the host, and perhaps also chocolates or a small gift for the hostess.

MANNERS

Generally speaking, the Batswana are not in the least aggressive, and violence is very seldom seen or heard in public society. Under the influence of alcohol, however, which is widely and easily available, voices rise, men often become more dominating and aggressive, and it is perhaps sensible to move quietly out of the way.

Many people will not make eye contact because they are too shy to do so. For the same reason, don't always expect a smile, especially in shops. The words "thank you" are not used as frequently as they might be in other societies, and it can sometimes be a source of irritation when small gifts and gratuities are taken without a word of thanks, but be assured that they will be very much appreciated. Without question, the general experience is that the Batswana are very polite, friendly, and warmly welcoming.

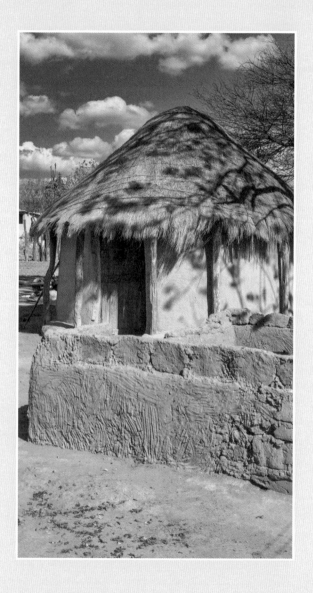

CHAPTER FIVE

PRIVATE *&* FAMILY LIFE

TRADITIONAL SOCIAL STRUCTURE

The heart of the traditional social structure in Botswana is in the rural village, which consists of a number of extended families. Here the core of such a family will be found, living together in a large and spacious "yard," among neighbors. There will usually be a male head of household and his wife and various huts for smaller children. When a daughter is about eighteen, a hut will be built specially for her, although she will leave to live with her husband when she marries. Sons will bring their wives to live in their parents' yard. Other relatives, usually of the senior male, may also live in the same yard. No one pays rent, although they are expected to contribute labor (helping with crops and stock, for example). Meals, provided by the head of the household, are free and are prepared and eaten in a central, usually outdoor, cooking area.

RURAL LIVING CONDITIONS

Traditional huts are round, and made of natural materials, typically wooden poles cut from trees in the nearby countryside and plastered with mud, or a mixture of mud and cow dung; conical roofs are mostly thatched. Increasingly cement block buildings with metal window frames and corrugated iron roofs are replacing the original huts. Such structures are hotter but more comfortable than the old-style dwellings. For government planning purposes a "village" is defined as a community containing more than 500 persons. All villages in Botswana now have a clinic and standpipes offering free, reliably drinkable, treated water. In many villages it is possible to have, at a cost, a standpipe in the

Family in front of their house in Moremi village in the Central District.

yard and, at a still greater price, water in the house itself. Not all villages have electricity (although many do), and those without are limited to battery radios, paraffin, and candles. Flush toilets are, obviously, only fitted in houses equipped with running water. In the cities and towns this is mostly the case, but in some city areas and in almost all rural villages the pit latrine (or "long drops") are the toilets of choice.

The traditional administrative hierarchy consists of headmen who are nominated by, and who report to, chiefs. All arguments and disputes requiring some form of resolution beyond the means of the parties involved must first be heard by a headman and cannot appear before a chief until this has been done. Very large villages are divided into wards, each ward having a headman.

DAILY LIFE AND ROUTINE IN A RURAL VILLAGE

People wake with the light. A chorus of birds, chickens, cockerels, goats, cows, and dogs will add to a slowly growing volume of sound that accompanies the start of any day. The morning meal will consist of tea and homemade bread (*diphaphatha*), which is made from flour, water, sugar, salt, and yeast over an outside wood fire. Ablutions will include a pit latrine and a bowl of

water. Children will walk to school for a 7:30 a.m. start.
They will be back at around 4:30 p.m., having had
lessons and sports through the day. Physical activities
vary but may include football, basketball, netball,
traditional dancing, and singing.

Depending on the season of the year, some will
walk to the family fields, which may be up to three
miles (five kilometers) away. It is the men who do the
plowing, using oxen or donkeys, but, if there is money,
some might be spent on renting a tractor. At harvest
time, women will go to the fields and cook there,
preparing *phaleche* (maize meal), *bogobe* (millet), or
morogo or *thepe* (green leaf vegetables). Meals are
eaten with the fingers. Workers will return home at
about 6:00 p.m. to find that the older children, having
returned from school, have cooked a similar meal
(perhaps replacing *phaleche* with *samp*, a coarsely
crushed maize meal). Food is served in communal
bowls, and shared by all. Men will sit on handmade
wooden stools. Women and children will sit on the
ground or on a skin.

If the family owns cattle they will be kept at the
cattle post, which could be very many miles away.
One or two individuals (the *badisa*, or helpers) will
be permanently resident there and responsible for
looking after the cattle, which range free without
restriction, held only by the need to return to the cattle
post for water. It is likely that the *badisas'* families will

Preparing the communal meal in the yard.

be with them, and it often happens that their children do not go to school. Payment for the *badisa*, who are not infrequently Bushmen, or San, is completely unregulated and depends on the wealth of the owner and the familial relationship with the employee, among other factors. Generally they are allowed to consume as much milk as they like and, in some areas, are presented with an adult cow once a year (which may then remain with the owner's herd). Commonly today a small monthly payment is made to the *modisa*, who spends it on tea and tobacco.

URBAN LIVING CONDITIONS

People in towns mostly live in "brick under tile," or brick under corrugated iron, single-story homes on serviced plots with piped water, electricity, and a sewerage connection. Gaborone, a "designer capital," has a deliberate arrangement of mixed "high," "medium," and "low-cost" housing, and an attractive system of pedestrian walkways between them.

Shopping

Shopping as a pastime is not an activity one would have associated with Botswana, even fifteen years ago, but times have changed and large, modern shopping malls have become the norm. Eighty percent of what is

In the Riverwalk Shopping Mall, Gaborone.

consumed in Botswana is imported, and you will find pretty well everything you need or want at a reasonable price. Most day-to-day consumer items are readily available in the larger centers. Gaborone's retail sector is expanding, its modern shopping areas stocking luxuries as well as the basics.

Supermarkets can be found in the larger towns, which will also have good clothing stores, liquor outlets, hardware shops, pharmacies, bookshops, and gift shops. In the larger centers, imported fresh vegetables can usually be purchased without difficulty. Mondays and days following public holidays may sometimes see temporary shortages of fresh items such as milk and vegetables.

Hours of trading are generally from 8:00 a.m. until 8:00 p.m., although liquor outlets open at 10:00 a.m. and close at 7:00 p.m., Monday to Saturday. Some shops, especially those in the smaller centers, close for an hour at lunchtime. Supermarkets in the larger centers open on Saturdays and Sunday mornings. There are many in Gaborone and in Francistown, and they are appearing in the tourist centers of Maun and Kasane. Typically, in the cities, malls include supermarkets, cinemas, and restaurants. The shops are mostly South African franchises selling food, fashion hardware, furniture, and fittings.

Shopping is a much more precarious business in small villages around the country. Almost every little center has its store and a bottle store or "liquor

Street vendors fill the gaps left by the shops.

restaurant." The range of goods in these outlets is sometimes amazing, at most times limited, but the basics will be available. Liquor stores usually restrict themselves to soft drinks, beer, and the cheaper spirits, but they are quite capable, occasionally, of unearthing an unexpected bottle of wine or a good whiskey!

At tourist destinations there are shops catering to the needs of visitors, with the usual array of crafts, books, and clothing.

Pay Day

For those in formal employment, pay day is close to or on the twenty-fifth of the month. The great majority of Batswana live on extended credit, and generally have no disposable income left on the following day.

FAMILY OCCASIONS

Older Batswana do not generally celebrate birthdays, although the new generation does. Older people, perhaps because their parents were illiterate, may know only the year of their birth, or may refer to it as being close in time to some notable or memorable event. For the most part, wedding anniversaries, Easter, or such occasions as Valentine's Day also go unmarked. Christmas, however, is an exception. Christmas Day and New Year's Day are widely celebrated. Modern tradition demands that each child is given a complete set of new clothing on each of the two days. Both days are marked as family days with attendance at church, music, parties, and the gathering of friends from near and far.

Weddings

Formerly, marriages were arranged by parents, and individuals were not allowed to marry unless they had passed through an initiation ceremony; but this is no longer the case. Nowadays, the man asks the woman to marry him, and if she agrees the prospective groom will inform his own parents. There will follow a long series of formal negotiations known as *patlo*, which lead to betrothal, and which will be confirmed by the groom's parents sending to the bride's family such gifts as an animal for slaughter, or dress materials, clothing, blankets, or shawls.

From this point onward, the procedure today is more like a conventional Western wedding, with engagement and wedding rings, a church service, reception, speeches, dancing, and wedding presents. If you are invited you are expected to bring a present; relatives, especially, are not excused from this duty. Gifts are usually kitchen or household items, not clothes; money is not generally given. There may be a kitchen "shower" for the bride-to-

be. Very rarely, there is a gift list available for
consultation.

Bride Price

It is the tradition among Batswana to compensate the
bride's parents for the loss of their daughter. The
payment is seen as a thanksgiving to the parents for
the care they have given to the girl's upbringing and
as a sign of gratitude for their kindness in now
allowing her husband to marry her. According to
Tswana law, no marriage is regarded as complete
unless the payment called *bogadi* has been made (it
is also known more generally throughout southern
Africa as *lobola*). A married woman with *bogadi* holds
a more honored position in society than one without.

Different tribes have different "rates," but the
payment is nearly always made in live cattle and
varies from four to twelve beasts. Around Mochudi,
for example, payment is fixed at four cows, while
among the people of Serowe the payment may be as
high as twelve animals. For the Kalanga people of
the north, payment in cattle is sometimes replaced
by the building of a hut for the prospective father-
in-law, or the gift of an overcoat. Strictly speaking,
bogadi should be paid before the wedding, but it is
often promised and delayed, and sometimes not
paid at all. The practice is increasingly falling away
in towns.

HIV/AIDS

Botswana has one of the highest HIV/AIDS
rates in the world. Almost every family has
been affected in some way by the pandemic.
The government has responded to this human
tragedy with a series of coordinated policies
aimed at education, treatment, care, and
support that has become a model for
combating AIDS.

Funerals

With AIDS there has been a vast increase in the
number of funerals. These traditionally took place on
Saturdays, but now fill both Saturdays and Sundays,
and sometimes Fridays and Wednesday afternoons. In
addition, social pressure is forcing poor families to pay
large amounts for expensive coffins, leaving survivors
even less well-off.

There are many differences in detail in the
methods and ritual used by different groups in
Botswana. In general, though, the body will be taken
at once to a mortuary and kept until the funeral. In
many cases, of course, there will be no mortuary, in
which case the body will be put in a coffin, covered
with wet sand, and kept for up to two days. Relatives
and neighbors will at once start cooking at the

deceased's residence in order to feed those who will be coming. The surviving spouse or parents will pay. A practice among some, following a death in a family, is for the curtains to be removed from all windows and the glass smeared with a mix of ash and water.

Word will go out to all relatives spread around the whole country, and outside it too, and they will be called to attend the funeral. Close relatives, such as a cousin or brother, must attend and, if they fail to do so, will have many negative things said about them. Visitors will call at the home from the moment of death to pay their respects: all visitors will pray, be invited to have a meal, and will then leave, although relatives from afar will stay; locals will visit daily.

Where possible the funeral will take place on a Saturday and so all visitors will be fed at least one meal a day for the whole week. To feed two or three hundred people over the course of a week is not exceptional, and the financial strain on the surviving spouse is very considerable. To some extent this will be ameliorated by a payment from a Burial Society, to which the family might have been subscribing for many years, or from an insurance policy, and from donations made by friends, working children, and relatives, but the survivor is very likely to be left with considerable costs to bear. It still happens in Botswana today that, on the day before the funeral, a senior relative will open a book in which he records the name and amount of money actually given by family, relatives, and visitors, which he collects on behalf of the surviving head of the family and hands over after the funeral. Seldom is this enough to cover the costs. Indeed, the cost of funerals today is unnecessarily high, and a significant social problem. Driven, perhaps, by the need to conform, to be recognized as "worthy," or to conserve status, families routinely spend huge amounts on a funeral that seriously impoverish the survivors.

The day before the funeral, the body will be brought from the mortuary by relatives, ideally in the evening, when more cooking starts in order to feed once more all the people who attend the funeral the following day. A cow will be killed for this feast.

Depending upon which church a surviving female spouse may belong to, she will be dressed in a particular color (usually blue or black) and will be required to wear only that color for the full mourning period—formerly a year, now more commonly one to six months. Traditionally, the widow could not sleep with a man until the mourning period had expired, and also, during that time, could not be greeted with a handshake.

At the service itself, speeches and eulogies are seen as very important and, if possible, the chief will also be present. It is seen as necessary to have a printed program of events lest the family be thought to be poor. The funeral procession starts from the deceased's yard and relatives carry the coffin. Plastic flowers will also be carried, and each bunch will have a message, which will be read. It used to be that if the surviving spouse was the widow, she had to join the procession wearing only one shoe, on the right foot, but this practice is not followed much today. When the coffin has been lowered into the grave relatives as a group will come forward, take a handful of soil, and throw it in. Previously flowers were strewn on the top of the grave, but now they are so frequently stolen that they are thrown in. All, especially men, are expected to help fill in the grave. On returning to the deceased's house there will be a large metal bath filled with water in which soak stems of *mosimama* (*Euphorbia* sp.). All hands and shovels must be washed in this water.

On the day following the funeral, some groups take all the deceased's clothing, rinse it in water, and dry it, after which a senior male, usually an uncle, will dispose of the property. Also on this day, the children and wife of the deceased will have their heads shaved. There is a lot of resistance to this today, especially from younger women, but the wife has no choice and must do it. Children and relatives will wear either a blue or black cloth tab on the left arm for a few months.

HOW LIFE IS CHANGING

A very important aspect of life in Botswana is the rate of social change, and for many, particularly the rural and the elderly, it is a frightening experience. Certainly the economy is growing, and there is more money around, as well as stores, shops, and tempting consumer items. At the same time traditional values are under severe attack—an attack spearheaded by the young. Raised, not in the village or to the natural rhythms of the seasons but in the glare of the television and the hurly-burly of town life, they see little to attract them in the past and imagine much waiting for them in the future; they have let go the former, and enthusiastically grasp the latter. The growing rift between young and old is slowly changing the nature of the social fabric, diminishing ties to tradition, weakening links between urban and rural, and rupturing relationships—all this to the dismay, concern, and sometimes confusion of a conservative population left in the past.

The younger generations in Botswana are as *au fait* with modern media and technology as their peers anywhere in the world. What divides them is education. The government education system has not been a great success. A very high percentage of the population, graduating from both the secondary and tertiary education systems, has been left poorly

Primary school concert.

equipped for the modern world. Private schools on the other hand, are exceptionally good but very expensive (the highest scoring in all Africa for "O" and "A" Level results is located in Gaborone!). The much smaller percentage of graduates from these schools is indistinguishable from their peers world-wide. Bought up with the ubiquitous smartphone and with access to Twitter, Facebook, YouTube, and satellite television, they march in lock step in interest and attitude with their international companions.

CHAPTER SIX

TIME OUT

Visitors who come to Botswana as tourists tend to have their leisure time planned for them, and will have very little opportunity to meet and mix with Batswana other than the staff of the lodge or hotel where they are staying. Experience suggests that people who come for a longer time will find, unless they make a concerted effort to the contrary, that their leisure time will be taken up with social events with people of similar cultural backgrounds to their own.

LEISURE

The Batswana are enormously sociable: they enjoy doing things together, with a lot of people in groups and loud music much in evidence. The way they spend their time depends entirely on their position in the social hierarchy. In the rural areas, where working hours are either nonexistent or totally flexible, the weekends are for drinking. Parties of men will gather under a shady tree in the village and drink a home-brewed beer made by the womenfolk during the week. There is nothing else to do.

In town, the Batswana spend much of their leisure time with friends, usually watching television in a noisy (to very noisy) group at a bar or in thousands at a football venue. At weekends they may drive out into the surrounding countryside and have a picnic. Those with cattle posts (which are likely to be a long distance away) will visit them once a month to check on the herd and perhaps pay the person looking after it. Increasingly, one sees Batswana walking for exercise.

Home activities center on the television set. Reading is not generally a leisure activity. Most people prefer to cook and eat at home; eating out at restaurants is becoming more common but, despite being by far the majority of the population, Batswana represent just a small fraction of the clientele at any restaurant.

ENTERTAINMENT

There is very little organized entertainment in the cities, even less in the towns, and nothing formal at all in the villages. Generally speaking, older Batswana prefer to

Church choir celebrating the translation of the Bible into the Nama language.

keep to themselves in their homes, or to visit their friends or their cattle posts. The younger generations tend to be less attracted to this idea. There are cinemas in the cities, and many bars and restaurants. For the young who have some discretionary income "going out" means meeting and drinking.

Choral singing is very popular among the Batswana. There are six or seven choirs in Gaborone, but they tend to sing at private functions or in churches on Sundays. Paid public performances are very rare indeed but traditionally, especially at Christmas in the rural villages, choirs meet and compete in day-long competitions. There is no dedicated theater in the country.

Left and above: The Kuru Dance Festival at Dqae Qare San Lodge, near Ghanzi.

Historically, dancing was an important element in tribal life and remains extremely popular. In the past, dancing troupes would have been found in every village. They are less in evidence today due to competition from more modern forms of entertainment. Traditionally dancers dressed in animal skins and troupes included either men or women in groups of ten to fifteen individuals. Tswana dancing is deeply connected to proudly held cultural values, and many efforts are made to keep the art alive and well. All government schools, from primary level upward, will have a dancing group and there are annual regional and national competitions such as the Domboshaba Cultural Festival and the Kuru Dance Festival. Often on public holidays, state or other special occasions, a popular group might be asked to perform.

SPORTS

Interest in football (soccer) completely dominates all other sports. Batswana watch it on television, read about it in newspapers, attend matches, and talk about it in bars. And there the interest in sports stops.

Undoubtedly this will change over time, but, for the moment, sports other than football are found mostly in the expatriate communities. Government schools encourage football and netball. Private schools coach cricket, rugby, basketball, swimming, and athletics but, after the school years, these sports are not widely supported nationally. Within expatriate groups, some cricket and rugby is kept alive, while from time to time there emerge, waxing and waning in popularity, such sports as cycling, motorcycle racing, and horse riding.

SHOPPING FOR PLEASURE

Short-term visitors are most likely to be tourists in places such as the two cities and Maun and Kasane—the starting points for the Okavango Delta and Chobe National Park respectively.

Traditional Batswana baskets.

While African curios are widely available in Botswana, the country itself produces little indigenous artwork—almost all of what you will see on sale is made elsewhere and imported from Zimbabwe, Congo, East Africa, or Malawi. One thing that Botswana does produce that is outstanding in terms of quality and value, and justifiably famous, is its baskets. These are handwoven and made almost exclusively in the Okavango region entirely from natural materials. They are genuine traditional artifacts that you will see in daily use in any village in the area. Thanks to the efforts of the National Museum and to commercial pressures, the quality of baskets on sale to visitors is extremely high. Being lightweight and of a reasonable size they are easy to

Ceramics and hangings in the markets of Maun.

pack and carry and, among other things, make wonderful wall decorations. Curio shops in all the tourist centers will sell them. The bigger shops in Maun, Kasane, and Gaborone will also offer the usual range of carvings in wood and stone, the latter being made from soapstone and mostly originating in Zimbabwe.

Another product for which Botswana has something of a reputation is the small mats and wall hangings woven from wool by a small group of women in a village called Oodi, 25 miles (40 km) north of Gaborone. A Norwegian couple started the project many years ago as a way for the village women to make some ready cash. Throughout its long history its prospects have fluctuated hugely, with production being spasmodic, slow, and unpredictable, and marketing and distribution almost nonexistent, but the quality has always been good. While such weaving is not a traditional art, the colorful products depicting village scenes have become something of a reminder of Botswana for those who have lived in the country.

The most visible evidence of traditional folk art can sometimes be found in the rural villages. Where round, thatched huts are still built and used, it is the custom occasionally to paint the smooth, mud-plastered walls and to decorate them. It is not the practice to use the bright colors and elaborate patterns favored by the Ndebele people in South Africa—the Batswana use dun colors and a few simple motifs.

Lolwapa walls surrounding a taditional house at Domboshaba heritage site.

More elaborate are the low, seldom more than waist-high, walls that enclose the courtyard in front of a dwelling. Called *lolwapa*, these walls, made from mud-plastered bricks, are often constructed with considerable pride and craftsmanship and can be quite striking. In Ngamiland, these walls are replaced among the Hambukushu people with high reed fences, beautifully made, and sometimes with intricate reed patterns built into them.

It is worth noting that travelers moving out of or into the Common Customs Area—South Africa, Swaziland, Lesotho, Botswana, and Namibia—may purchase goods at duty-free shops (those in Johannesburg and Cape Town are excellent), but people traveling regionally inside the CCA may not.

Bargaining

Curios and mementos can be bought in two distinctly different ways: either in formal shops on the street, in hotels, and in lodges; or from itinerant hawkers and roadside displays. In the former, items will be priced, and where this is done bargaining is not an option. Items from the latter will not be priced and you most definitely should bargain and, indeed, are expected to do so.

Some visitors are uneasy about doing this, feeling that they are depriving the seller of hard-earned money to which he is fairly entitled. Often people coming from a hard currency area will find the item ridiculously inexpensive, even at the offered price. These are fair reactions, but it is important to bear one or two other considerations in mind. You can be sure the seller knows much more about the current exchange rates than you do; observing your dress, accent, face, and accoutrements, he will have a very good idea of where you are from and how much you are likely to pay; his asking price is based upon his expectation that you will bargain; and, finally, you cannot force him to sell, so if he accepts your price, whatever he says, he is happy to do so.

What is your best strategy? There is no one answer to this question: successful bargaining is an art developed over time. Experience in Botswana shows that an active sense of humor and willingness to share laughter is a vital ingredient in any transaction. In response to the seller's initial request some histrionics displaying shock and horror at the high price is a good first move, accompanied by a response of somewhere between a quarter and a third of his offer. From this point on you must play it by ear. If you find yourselves at a dead end and you think the price reached is still too high, walk away and be seen to be actively negotiating with neighboring sellers. Time is an essential ingredient in the game, and how much of it you have to spare will play a significant part in your success.

CURRENCY AND MONEY CHANGING

Botswana's unit of currency is the pula, whose value is linked to a basket of four international currencies and the South African rand. In 2019 there were approximately 13 to 14 pula to the pound sterling, and 10 to 11 to the US dollar: rates change from time to time. Pula note denominations are 10, 20, 50, 100, and 200, with the largest coin being 5 pula. The pula is made up of 100 thebe.

Visitors from the subregion will find Botswana expensive. Bureaux de change are found in the larger centers, at some of the bigger border posts, and at Sir Seretse Khama International Airport, while traveler's checks and foreign currency can be changed at all banks, throughout the week and on Saturday mornings.

International Credit Cards

The use of credit cards in Botswana is now widespread. Most travel agents, hotels, and safari operators can and do accept credit cards, as do pharmacies, supermarkets, shops, gas stations, and the like. Using an international credit card, it is possible to withdraw cash from ATMs, which are widely found in all cities and towns.

Banks

The country's four main commercial banks are Barclays Bank of Botswana Ltd., Standard Chartered Bank of Botswana Ltd., First National Bank of Botswana Ltd., and Stanbic Bank of Botswana Ltd. They provide high branch coverage backed up by agencies and ATMs in the major centers. Banks are not open on public holidays. Normal opening times are generally 8:30 or 9:00 a.m. to 3:30 p.m. daily, and between about 8:30 a.m. and 11:00 a.m. on Saturdays.

Be warned that banking can be a time-consuming business in Botswana, especially at the end of the month, with very long, slow-moving lines. In shops, foreign currencies will not be accepted over the counter. Generally speaking, hotels and tourist shops will accept US dollars, but will also take care not to lose over the exchange rate! In addition to cash withdrawal, ATMs today allow for the depositing of cash and the settlement of certain local accounts.

Bank agencies, those offering limited services in the smaller towns around the country, do not always observe standard hours of business, are open for shorter periods, and are often closed on Saturdays. Agencies maintain current and savings accounts and will cash traveler's checks. They do not, however, deal in foreign currencies, apart from the South African rand, except by special arrangement. They issue foreign exchange and traveler's checks only by special arrangement.

RESTAURANTS AND LOCAL FOOD

The new middle classes and the expatriate community form the bulk of the restaurant clientele. Mostly it is couples, occasionally small groups, and these are usually there for a change, or perhaps for a celebration.

The cities and tourist areas are well supplied with restaurants and, in the former, a wide choice of Italian, Indian, and Thai food is available, along with the traditional steak houses. As you move away from the capital the choice diminishes but standards will remain perfectly acceptable.

You will not find "local" food in a smart restaurant in the bigger towns. It is in the smaller towns and villages, however, where visitors can run into a little trouble. There, the words "restaurant" and "café" are liberally used, and visitors responding to such signs may find the standards of hygiene and choice of menu to be less than desirable.

FOOD AND DRINK

Foreign visitors may well find the local cuisine limited, unimaginative, or not entirely to their taste. Most Batswana like beef on the bone and prefer tough meat, as opposed to tender cuts such as fillet. Underdone meat is not popular. The nearest to a traditional meat

Traditional Kalanga cooking in northeastern Botswana.

dish would be *seswaa*, which is beef boiled in huge cast-iron pots and pounded to a stringy mass. It is often eaten with *morogo*, a mix of local spinach, tomatoes, and onions. To Western tastes the dish is very fatty, but locally it is very popular, especially for weddings, funerals, and other big events.

Although salt is used in cooking, the use of spices is very limited. For this reason, foreigners often find traditional Tswana dishes bland. Everyday fare would include either ground sorghum or corn as a staple, with *morogo*. If meat is available, well-cooked boiled meat is common; meat on the bone is preferred, oxtail is a favorite, and chicken is becoming more popular. Sour milk is a popular beverage.

Changing Tastes

Our Motswana friend's mother will not eat chicken, as she says she does not feel she has eaten anything much after such a meal, and prefers a large chunk of well-cooked beef on the bone. Her daughter eats chicken, believes too much red meat is not good for her, tries to cut down on starches, and knows the importance of eating lots of vegetables. Her own daughter rushes home and makes herself a bowl of pasta with a nice sauce!

In establishments that cater to tourists, the situation is very different. A wide range of cuisines more familiar to Western palates will be on offer, with special emphasis on African meats and fish. These might include warthog (delicious despite its name), kudu, impala, ostrich, and crocodile (also delicious, tasting of lobster or crab). In the Okavango and Chobe areas you will be offered bream, a freshwater fish caught locally and a total delight.

Western-style beer is by far the most popular alcoholic drink, with wine second, and spirits a more distant third. While drunkenness is a serious problem in the country—especially on the road—a surprisingly large percentage of the populace do not drink alcohol at all and prefer soft drinks and fruit juices (this is voluntary, and religious in origin). In the rural areas traditional beer (*khadi*) is brewed and drunk in the villages. This is made to various local recipes starting with sorghum or maize, and comes at various alcoholic strengths. The brewing and selling of local beer, especially in rural areas, is an important source of income for some families. A commercial variant of one of the more innocuous brews, Chibuku, is made in the towns and widely distributed.

TIPPING

There are no fixed rules for tipping. The Batswana generally do not do it, or leave a very small amount. Westerners are guided by, but do not strictly follow, a 10 percent rule of thumb. In hotels all expenses go "on the bill," and it is not usual, when checking out and paying at the reception desk, to leave any tip there. In safari lodges much the same arrangement is followed, but it is more common there to leave a tip—usually in foreign currency—for the guides who spent hours with you either on game drives or game walks, and a lesser amount for the general staff who really do go out of their way to give you outstanding and excellent service.

Table Manners

These depend on where you are and whom you are with. The masses are not necessarily familiar with the refined manners of a Western dining room. While the younger generation, as with everything in Botswana, is growing up with norms and patterns of behavior different from their parents, and is much more Western in orientation, you might still find yourself lunching in a restaurant with a businessman who is holding a large bone in both hands, gnawing at it and speaking at the same time. It would be extraordinarily rude even to hint at any surprise.

It is most unusual to see a chair pulled out or a door held open for a lady.

TOURIST DESTINATIONS

Botswana is synonymous with diamonds and big game. Although tours of the diamond mines can be, and are, arranged, the mines themselves are remote and not on the current tourist routes, and so such visits are usually for people living in the country.

Big game is more accessible and very much at the core of the country's burgeoning tourist industry. The two main centers are Maun and Kasane, the former giving access to the Okavango, and the latter to Chobe National Park. The current practice is for people to

Sightseeing boat on the Cuando River in Chobe National Park.

book safaris with established safari camps in one or both of these regions, and to travel from one to the other by light aircraft. The game areas of Botswana are divided into concessions that are all leased out by local government and are not accessible to individual members of the public driving in their own or hired vehicles. The only areas to which the public has access are the national parks and game reserves. It is therefore difficult for foreign visitors to see Botswana's game other than by paying quite expensive rates to one or more safari lodges, or by staying at camp sites in the parks.

It must be said that the standard of accommodation, food, and service in Botswana's lodges is absolutely world-class, and the experience unparalleled. Most game viewing will be done from open vehicles, but some safari companies offer game walks, which, in the opinion of many, is the only way to really see and

Transporting goods by *mokoro* at the Kazungula border crossing.

experience the wild and its animals. A visit to the
Delta will include not only game but a chance to
travel in a *mokoro* (a wooden dugout canoe). This is
an authentic Okavango experience: one slides silently
through narrow passages in the papyrus, or across
tranquil lagoons under the watchful eyes of a herd of
elephants. It is something never to be forgotten, wet
seat and all!

There are other sights in Botswana besides its
game. Tsodilo Hills has more than five thousand
individual rock paintings on four hundred separate
sites. It is a World Heritage site, but there is no lodge
there, although it can easily be reached from
Shakawe, at the western extremity of the Delta.
Drotsky's Caves are a series of dolomite caverns that

Rock paintings in the Tsodilo Hills, attributed to the San people.

are absolutely spectacular but, being exceedingly remote and utterly undeveloped, require visitors to be locally based or to have a lot of money in order to arrange a special expedition.

There is a single safari lodge in Makgadikgadi Pans, where game itself is not the main attraction. These salt pans are the remains of a once-vast lake that covered more than 47,000 square miles (120,000 sq. km) of northern Botswana. Featureless and windswept, without a tree or a blade of grass, it is a stunningly beautiful place, presenting a kaleidoscope of colors that amazes the senses. This camp is one of the few from which one can visit a local cattle post.

So-called ecotourism, which many understand to mean actually entering the villages of local people,

Baobab trees on Kubu Island in the Makgadikgadi Pan.

has not been taken on with much enthusiasm in
Botswana. This is possibly because the Batswana
guides are not keen to show the less salubrious side
of their country and don't really understand its
attractions compared to that offered by a pride of
lions or a herd of elephant.

Wildlife

In the 1950s and '60s hunting was Botswana's sole
tourisim related activity; it remained a small facet of
the rapidly growing industry in post-independence
times as wonderful lodges sprang up in the Okavango
and Chobe regions. However, one of the first acts of
the former president and ardent conservationist, Ian
Khama, in 2010, was to ban all forms of hunting. In
2019 his successor, President Masisi, revoked the ban

on hunting elephant. How much further this revocation might be taken is presently unknown, and a worldwide controversy has been ignited. Conservationists will be infuriated but the issue is not a clear-cut one at all.

No one can be certain about how many elephant there are in Botswana: they range widely between Zimbabwe and Botswana and to a lesser extent into Angola. Published figures vary. A current and conservative estimation puts the stock at some 160,000 animals. Typically their population will increase at between 3 and 5 percent per annum. Taking a very conservative figure of 3 percent annual growth yields just under 5,000 new elephants every year. Already conflicts between man and elephant are increasing and a common view is that that rate of growth cannot be sustained in the country. It is one thing for conservationists abroad to cry out—but it is not their crops that are being destroyed nor their

villages being damaged. There are no easy answers to this question, but it is the Batswana's problem and they must resolve it as they see fit.

In the past, licenses were strictly controlled by the Department of Wildlife and National Parks (DWNP) and were given out annually after a careful assessment of the available wildlife resource. The number of animals actually removed by hunting was very small indeed. For example, licenses for slightly more than one hundred elephants were given out in the last pre-ban year. Not all were shot, and that number is infinitesimal compared to the annual crop of some four to five thousand new elephants that are born each year.

Thanks to the efforts of NGOs (Nongovernmental Organizations) and DWNP, there is a growing

awareness among the Batswana of the importance and value of wildlife. With generous American financial support, a program known as CBNRM (Community Based Natural Resource Management) is currently being put in place, but is experiencing severe difficulties. The program seeks to encourage local communities to work with investors from the tourism sector in developing lodges and tourist activities. The difficulties arise from the complete absence of any business experience or any understanding of how businesses work on the part of the local community. There is a desire to get rich quickly and to be rewarded at unrealistically high levels, and a failure to understand the importance of a stable, long-term business relationship.

CHAPTER SEVEN

TRAVEL, HEALTH, & SAFETY

AIR BOTSWANA

Air Botswana, the national carrier, is perpetually in the throes of privatization, but at the time of writing remains a government parastatal. It operates a small fleet of aircraft that serves four destinations in the country—Francistown, Gaborone, Kasane, and Maun—and makes international connections to Johannesburg, Cape Town, and Windhoek. Flights to Lusaka in Zambia and Harare in Zimbabwe are expected soon. The list of external destinations tends to change from time to time, so it is important to check on the current situation. The only long-distance international flights that leave from or arrive in Botswana are those of Ethiopian Air.

Commercial light aircraft companies service the safari industry around the Okavango Delta, linking with the Air Botswana network.

GETTING AROUND

Botswana has a network of world-class paved roads joining all the cities, towns, and major villages: bus services serve them all. For still smaller destinations and for local journeys the ubiquitous "combi" (a multiseater passenger van) meets the need. Every destination will have a "bus rank" from which all transportation starts out and where it all ends up. They are generally filled with a wild melée of buses, taxis, combis, touting conductors, and confused passengers. The words "scheduled departure" have little meaning here, but people are extremely friendly, really helpful (especially to obvious foreigners), and buses will generally leave "when they are full." The vehicles used today are very modern with air-conditioning, toilets, and very reasonable fares. For visiting youngsters in particular the excitement and adventure of a long-distance bus journey in Botswana is something that shouldn't be missed.

Royal Progress

There are differing estimates as to exactly how many miles of paved road existed in the country at independence in 1966. Figures range from four to eight miles (seven to thirteen kilometers)! Whatever the correct figure, it is certain that part of this was a single mile in early Francistown, with the rest dating to the visit of King George VI, Queen Elizabeth, and their two daughters in 1947. The program required that the royal party travel from Lobatse railway station to the airport—a distance of around seven miles (about ten kilometers)—and it was not considered dignified for them to do so on anything other than the best road surface available. So Lobatse gained what was for years its only paved road!

ROADS AND TRAFFIC

Vehicles drive on the left-hand side of the road. Road traffic rules generally accord with international requirements. The use of seat belts in the front and rear seats of the vehicle is compulsory, as is the need to carry a driver's license with you when driving. International driver's licenses are valid and national licenses allow a person to drive for six months in

Botswana. The police are not especially sympathetic regarding driver's licenses and sometimes, if caught driving without carrying one, drivers are both fined and refused permission to drive the vehicle further until in actual possession of the license. This can mean that, if no one else in the vehicle has a license and can drive, the vehicle is impounded until the license is produced.

Currently Botswana has more than 4,300 miles (7,000 km) of excellent paved road, all of it built to, and maintained at, international standards, and another 2,560 miles (4,100 km) of maintained gravel roads. And there are thousands of miles of bush tracks that are maintained only by regular usage. In addition the country now has in excess of 550,000 vehicles.

Driving Habits and Pedestrians
By and large, most Batswana are country people who are not very traffic conscious and don't have good road sense. It is possibly for this reason that, by world standards, Botswana has an exceedingly high accident rate. Compounding this is the fact that cattle, donkeys, and goats roam the main roads and city streets and are a major contributor to the accident and death rates. Driving long distances at night demands extra special care, and is not recommended. Those who have to do so go to the trouble of buying and fitting a very good set of high-powered spotlights on their vehicle.

Driving under the influence of alcohol is another major cause of accidents. There are rules against drinking and driving, but they do not appear to be enforced. Certainly in the cities and towns the extent of this problem is amply demonstrated by the number of flattened traffic lights, delineator posts, and streetlights, especially noticeable on Saturday and Sunday mornings! Traffic lights should be treated with extreme caution at all times of day and night, as many drivers will take chances, not only on the amber lights, but on the red as well.

It is not just drivers who may be influenced by alcohol: there are often drunk pedestrians about, whose behavior may be unpredictable. People often step out on to the road suddenly and without looking, so special care is required. Also, they may be hard to see at night, although there is good lighting in the town centers.

INTERCITY TRAVEL

Trains and Buses
Botswana Railways operates the rail service on the single north–south line that runs through the country from Cape Town in South Africa to Lusaka in Zambia and Dar es Salaam in Tanzania, and along which two trains travel daily, but only as far as Bulawayo. Travel is slow, with many stops, but inexpensive, and,

Intercity bus in Ngamiland District, northwest Botswana.

depending upon the class chosen, reasonably comfortable: first class has air-conditioning. First and second-class compartments for six are unlikely to have more than a few people in them, and normal conversation is possible provided the language barrier does not intervene.

Buses connect all the major centers with a fairly efficient and certainly low-cost service. Schedules may exist for long-distance buses but drivers are much more inclined just to leave when the bus is full. Some of the vehicles are quite luxurious, comfortable, and very modern; some will have a video player suspended from the roof at the front of the bus and delight their passengers with endless Westerns or kickboxing movies! It is most unlikely that any presentation will hold your attention for long, which is perhaps as well, as attempting to listen to the dialogue above the roar of the engine and the sound of the wind through the open windows is a challenge. All towns have a central bus depot; it is from here that services will depart, and it is here that enquiries about the service must be made.

LOCAL TRANSPORTATION

Taxis and Combis

There is no formal mass transportation system in any town or city. In the larger towns and cities, taxis are becoming much more common and can be summoned by phone. Be warned, though: they do not have meters and the fare is the subject of some negotiation. Every ride is a different price and the only advice is to ask a local for guidelines at your starting point. Until one is familiar with the routine it is as well to have local help in this regard. Tipping is entirely a matter of discretion (see page 131).

The masses travel in what are known as "combis," owned and run by licensed private individuals. These fourteen-seater minibuses do not operate to a timetable, although they follow set routes and are subject to some regulation. Although there are some regulated stopping places—and combis certainly stop there—they also stop almost anywhere else. Apart from the designated stops there are no signposts and no published routes, so the system can be used only after appropriate local knowledge has been acquired. That said, however, it is inexpensive, fast, and efficient, from the passenger's point of view. Other motorists may have a different opinion. Combi drivers are masters of the unexpected: they may stop suddenly and without warning, overtake on the left, drive over sidewalks, cut across in front of another vehicle. and commit any of numerous violations. Your only defense is to be forewarned and careful!

Catching the bus to Gaborone at the Boatle interchange.

Tourist resort at Kasane, at the confluence of the Chobe and Zambezi Rivers.

WHERE TO STAY

All towns have hotels. In the cities these will be of international standard and, in the smaller centers, of a perfectly acceptable local standard. In the tourist areas, of course, there are innumerable lodges and campsites. Increasingly these are being successfully organized and run in conjunction with local African communities.

Bed and Breakfasts are a relatively new phenomenon and are well regulated and reliable. They are to be found only in the two cities and in one or two major towns. Often they are not very much less expensive than their hotel competitors. A relatively new phenomenon is the appearance of Airbnb. Many have registered with this organization and, adhering to its strict rules, provide good alternatives to the more expensive hotels. All these accommodation options are readily discovered via an Internet search.

HEALTH MATTERS

HIV/AIDS

Without question, this is the scourge of southern Africa. Different statistics abound, and are often not comparable. Suffice it to say, however, that in all the countries of the region HIV/AIDS is having a devastating effect on economies and social structure. In 2019 it was reported that nearly 25 percent of Batswana between the ages of fifteen and fifty were HIV positive—roughly 17 percent of the total population. AIDS is ripping apart the fabric of families in this country and producing generations of orphans. It is reported that the economic cost accounts for a significant portion of the country's development budget. Anti-retrovirals (ARVs) are distributed free to the approximately 140,000 individuals exhibiting symptoms and receiving treatment. Despite the disease being widely acknowledged within the country, rates of infection are still worryingly high, especially among the younger generation. A major success has been the almost total elimination of mother-to-child infections.

HIV/AIDS is not communicated by touching, and visitors may be assured that waiters, taxi drivers, shop assistants, and the like are not going to infect them. What is certain, however, is that the disease is rife, particularly among prostitutes, and that unprotected sex must be avoided.

Malaria

Parts of Botswana do fall into the malarial area. Mosquitoes transmit malaria, and do not generally survive intense cold. Thus in the south of the country, including around Gaborone and some way north, malaria is not a problem because the winter frost kills off the mosquitoes. In the north, however, where rainfall is higher, temperatures are generally higher and the winters are not as cold, malaria is an issue. The type of malaria most commonly encountered is *falciparum*, one of the complications of which is cerebral malaria, a very serious condition indeed. This is not a different kind of malaria, merely an advanced state of the disease. Acting quickly dramatically diminishes the threat of this particular condition.

People who live in malarial areas in Botswana generally do not take prophylactics: to do so lifelong is impractical, tedious, and, because of the possibility of long-term harm, is seen as unhealthy. Such people tend rather to take sensible steps to reduce the possibility of being bitten. They wear long sleeves, long pants, and cover their feet after sunset. They sleep under mosquito nets and expose themselves as little as possible. Knowing the symptoms well, they take a treatment if they are infected.

It is not wise for the visitor to follow this course. Certainly you should take all the sensible precautions that reduce the chances of being bitten, but you should have the additional protection of a recommended prophylactic, of which there are a great many. In making a choice, it is important to know that Chloroquine-resistant strains of malaria are now common in Botswana, and to take this into account.

Other Health Risks

Bilharzia, or Schistosomiasis, is an ever-present threat in Africa, and Botswana, despite its reputation as a desert country, is no exception. As a general rule, you should assume that all rivers, streams, and dams are infected, although not heavily. This is also true of the Okavango, especially around populated areas. The only way to avoid contracting the disease is not to bathe or wade in water. Curiously, bilharzia cannot be caught by drinking untreated, infected water. Saliva is sufficient to prevent contamination. Symptoms take at least six weeks to develop, and the disease is easily cured today.

Sleeping sickness, or Trypanosomiasis, is a disease transmitted by the bite of an infected tsetse fly, and is a much-reduced threat in modern Botswana. At its widest extent it occurs only in Ngamiland: in the Ngami, Okavango, Mababe, and Chobe areas. The fly can inflict a painful bite and, if you should contract the disease, its symptoms, including headaches and a fever, develop only after about two weeks. A blood test can confirm if a patient is suffering from sleeping sickness. The condition is easily cured.

Rabies is endemic in many wild animal populations in Botswana (and, of course, in unvaccinated dogs), but cases remain very rare. Its presence is often marked by unusual behavior, such as an unprovoked attack on a human, or unusual friendliness. If a suspected rabid creature bites, it is vitally important to get the patient to a hospital as soon as possible. A treatment is available that involves only five injections and is extremely effective if administered quickly enough after the bite—that is, within twenty-four hours. If this is not done, death will result. Strange as it may seem, the most effective immediate first aid is to wash the wound with soap and water: soap kills the virus. Any soap will do, including dishwashing liquid. There is now a vaccination, but a rabid bite must still be treated.

Tick-bite fever affects many people, especially newcomers to the country and, therefore, visitors. It is prevalent in the rainy season, particularly in March and April, and is passed on to humans from the bite of a tiny, pinhead-sized tick, especially common in grasslands. The disease incubates for seven days and then manifests itself. The symptoms include severe aching of the bones, headache, backache, and fever. Although it can be serious and exceedingly unpleasant, it is a self-limiting disease and will run its course in three or four days. Typically, other symptoms include swollen and painful glands. It's nearly always possible to locate an infected bite—the site will be marked by a raised yellow head with a small, black, central spot. The disease is easily controlled through a course of tetracycline.

The sun in the Kalahari is fierce, and those whose skins are not used to it should wear hats and apply sunburn creams, especially the kind with ultraviolet screening properties. Dust in the dry season can irritate eyes, so an eyewash solution is a good idea. Mild attacks of diarrhea are not uncommon; Lomotil, a nonprescription medicine, is an effective cure.

Medical Facilities
Botswana is well served by hospitals and health centers. General hospitals are located in all the major centers. Many villages throughout the country have medical clinics staffed by trained personnel. Some are in radio contact with hospitals. Medical Rescue International (operating in Botswana since 1991) offers immediate, professional help in emergencies.

Drinking Water
Water in the towns and villages, reassuringly, is perfectly safe to drink.

Vaccinations
Visitors wanting to take sensible precautions should be vaccinated against hepatitis A and B, which are common diseases, before entering the country. An alternative is an injection of immunoglobulin that will provide protection for about three months. It is also advisable to have tetanus and typhoid boosters. By all accounts the risk is extremely low, but it may be as well for foreigners to be on the safe side. Venereal infections are quite common, especially gonorrhea. Currently, yellow fever inoculation certificates are not required unless one is visiting from an African country north of the Zambezi, or from Angola or northern Namibia, where the fever is endemic. Inoculation should take place at least ten days before entering Botswana, and it is valid for ten years.

COVID-19

In early 2020 the Covid pandemic reached Botswana and the government responded rapidly with a lockdown. When this began to be eased and schools started to reopen, the sale of tobacco and alcohol remained prohibited. Given a largely unsophisticated population with a penchant for social interaction, there was a very high risk of a tsunami of infections, especially with the constant interchange of goods and people with neighboring South Africa. However, the lockdown taught people the importance of wearing a mask at all times and of keeping to the social distance rules, with the result that the infection rate was remarkably low. Had the feared tsunami happened the health system would surely have been completely overwhelmed.

CRIME

Botswana is a country with an ever-widening gap between rich and poor, with high unemployment, and troubled by innumerable, illegal, and mostly desperate refugees. There is crime. The commonest form is petty in nature, and tends to be opportunistic—the theft of handbags and cell phones, and pickpocketing. Home invasion is also common, with the targets usually televisions, videos, computers, jewelry, money, cameras, and cell phones. More violent crime does occur: vehicle hijacks are extremely rare but have happened; bank robberies have also been reported; rape also happens and is common among Batswana. Crime is an ever-present threat, but not enough to worry unduly about. Most households that can afford it have an alarm system connecting them to a local security company and there is a growing incidence of electric fences around homes. Exercising simple precautions dramatically reduces the risk of crime: lock cars and houses, guard handbags, button pockets, and don't leave temptation in the way of others. There are no "no go" areas in Botswana: one simply requires some common sense about not exposing oneself to unnecessary risks.

Firearms are strictly controlled in Botswana: no weapon may be owned without a permit, and only a limited number of permits are issued each year. To be in possession of a firearm without a permit is considered an extremely serious offense. There is a total restriction on the importation of side arms, automatic weapons, and small-bore (.22 caliber, for example) rifles. An import permit is required for any weapon allowed into the country. A permit may be obtained by writing in advance to The Officer in Charge, Central Arms Registry, P/Bag 0012, Gaborone; tel. 3951161 ext. 2466.

CHAPTER EIGHT

BUSINESS BRIEFING

BUSINESS CULTURE

At government level and among corporations, business tends to be formal and very much relationship-based. The business community is, due to the relatively small size of the economy, completely dominated by government, but there is a thriving private sector, composed mostly of Batswana, including many of Indian origin and a considerable proportion of expatriates.

The workforce is almost exclusively Batswana, whose interests are cared for by extensive, modern labor legislation that controls working hours, minimum wages, leave (including maternity leave), safety and health issues, and so on. There are also nascent trade union organizations of varying effectiveness.

THE "ELDERS"

For many years after Botswana became independent it suffered from a chronic shortage of skilled personnel in every conceivable field. As far as government was concerned, in those early days, anyone who had a degree of any sort was guaranteed a job in the new administration; school diplomas were also rare and much sought after. Now, some fifty-five years after independence, many of the government's first recruits are still employed and some have reached very senior positions, keeping with them the values and traditions of their times. Batswana refer to such people as *Moswa o eme*, a phrase used to describe the big, old, dead trees that they leave standing in their fields, it being harder to remove them than to let them remain where they are! Such individuals, when encountered, will not respond to the flurry and hurry that is sometimes the way of modern business. They must be treated with quiet respect, tolerated, and not shown up, for they will be powerful, well-connected, and well-respected. Whatever the cost, they call the shots; you will dance to their tune.

OFFICE ETIQUETTE

In public spaces in a business environment, where one is on show, the emphasis will be on politeness, formality, and, particularly, on correct procedure. A receptionist will ask your business and invite you to sit while she locates the person you have come to see. Either you will be directed to that person's office or they will come to meet you. The actual meeting will take place either in a convenient meeting room or in the individual's office. Unless the matter is very brief you will be offered tea or coffee. The coffee will almost always be instant, and the tea will either be a standard variety or Rooibos, a very popular herbal tea. Often the milk will be powdered. Handshakes precede and follow such meetings.

MEETINGS

It sometimes seems as if the Batswana are professional meeting holders: it is easy to get the impression that meetings dominate all other kinds of economic activity. If, for example, one is trying to speak to a particular individual by telephone, it's very likely that the person will be "in a meeting." What that actually means obviously varies, but it may cover any activity ranging from a legitimate formal meeting to slipping out to do some shopping. That aside, however, the Batswana do get involved in a great many meetings. The number, duration, and frequency of meetings, especially in the public sector, has been raised almost to an art form. Meetings are often prolonged by the belief that all must have their say, regardless of whether the point being made has already been made, perhaps more than once already.

While getting ideas and debating options is obviously wise, it can happen that a meeting is protracted and the subjects discussed are trivial. Sometimes meetings appear to provide a cover for lack of experience, judgment, and self-confidence, and help to create a comfortable feeling of shared responsibility.

A Prayerful Meeting

It is not unusual for someone to suggest that, "This meeting should start with a prayer." There will be a mumbled murmur of assent, and the speaker will pronounce a short prayer. Once a brave soul had the temerity to question this and ask, "What about any Muslims, Buddhists, agnostics, or other religions that might be present?" This set off a forty-two-minute debate on whether there should be a prayer, in what religion, and what to do about the nonreligious present. No resolution to this debate was in sight when (thankfully) one individual stood up, unasked, softly pronounced a short payer under his breath, and sat down again. The meeting moved on.

A related issue is the matter of leaving messages to call back for those "in meetings." This can be extremely frustrating, as often the message is not written down, not written down properly, or not passed on to the individual concerned; or, more rarely, the individual does not bother to return the call. Leaving messages is not a dependable method of making contact with another person.

Missing Meetings

As we have seen (on pages 56–7), attitudes toward meetings and appointments are not what one might expect. Appointments are routinely cancelled, forgotten completely, or changed at the last minute. It is essential to be prepared for this eventuality; so, to avoid wasted time and effort, it is advisable to confirm every appointment in advance—not only the day before, but also a few hours before.

APPEARANCE AND BUSINESS DRESS

The Batswana themselves are very particular about dress in a business situation. Smartness, style, and careful grooming are seen as important, and men will almost invariably wear suits and ties. As elsewhere, as one moves away from the larger corporate entities there is less and less formality and, at the manufacturing

Representatives of Botswana and India discuss cooperation in the field of MSMEs.

level, for example, anything goes. The Batswana, however, have very clear ideas about the links between appearance, status, and importance—important people and important events. This is partly driven by traditional values—one must show respect—but it is also about status and what other people might think of you. For example, no Motswana would go to a funeral in anything but his or her best clothes; they would not dream of visiting a Permanent Secretary in anything but a smart suit and tie, and they would always want to look their best in public.

PUNCTUALITY

For a people whose traditional lives were, until relatively recently, regulated by the seasons and the daily passage of the sun, being punctual, or being concerned about time, does not now appear to have the highest priority. Having a different view about the importance and management of time is probably one of the greatest hurdles that visiting foreigners must overcome. It is very unusual that anything starts precisely on time. Generally speaking, meetings start late, and people often arrive later still. Transportation difficulties may well help to account for this, but it is perfectly normal for all kinds of events to start late. Weddings and funerals, for example, may run as much as an hour or two behind schedule; concerts and shows can be relied upon to start at least ten minutes late.

Better Late Than Never: A Caution for Visitors!

It is the widespread habit in Botswana to refer to a deceased person as "Late"—the late Mr. Somole, for example. It is also an equally widely used habit to employ the word late in its more usual sense. This can lead to some blackly amusing situations: "Where is Monica? We need to get this meeting started." "Ah! Monica, sadly, she is late!" One needs to tread cautiously here until one discovers exactly what kind of "lateness" is being spoken of.

BUSINESS ENTERTAINING

Lunch is by far the most usual means of formal entertaining in the business world. Business breakfasts are rare but do occasionally happen, especially for quite large groups being addressed by a visiting speaker. Lunches tend to follow morning board meetings. In the case of large-scale national and international conferences, all government employees and invited guests will expect to be provided with tea in the morning and afternoon as well as lunch and something (always non-alcoholic) to drink with it. Entertaining at home is unusual except among the expatriate community.

CONFRONTATION

Situations involving confrontation are extremely rare among the Batswana, because the risks are seen to be very high: confrontation might spark anger, resentment, or resistance. Anger and irritation are nearly always very well controlled and concealed. The Batswana try to avoid any kind of criticism that they sense will lead to confrontation. It is not part of the culture to display these or any other emotions, apart from humor, too readily, and this fact has some interesting consequences.

Direct criticism using pointed, blunt terms would not be well received. Terms such as "fool," "foolish," or "idiot" would be taken very seriously. Using bad language at the same time would add insult to injury. The Batswana are not used to it. It is not the "Botswana Way," and such behavior is anathema to the people of this country. It would not provoke a similar response, but would be more likely to cause a deep, resentful silence, and might set in motion a long-term and hidden vengeful retaliation.

Perhaps most pervasively, wanting to avoid confrontation impacts adversely on the general quality of supervision (see below), while, on the positive side, it makes for a peace-loving community and nation where people make an effort to get on with each other without hostility and aggression getting in the way.

SUPERVISION

In the field of management, supervisory skills are not a strong point. Getting people to do what they are supposed to do often involves, at one level or another, a face-to-face situation where the failure to meet agreed upon performance standards is discussed openly and frankly. Elsewhere, this is not normally a difficult situation to manage, but to the Motswana supervisor it appears threatening, as he or she will be accusing another of not performing adequately and, no matter how this is done or how things are said, it will be seen by both parties as being critical and confrontational.

The tendency is to avoid such a situation in the first place by not using specifics, by staying away from hard facts, by avoiding accusation, and by relying instead on implication and allusion to convey meaning. As a consequence, the lack of clarity often confuses the issues further and makes subsequent follow-up even more difficult. Management training is available and appropriate courses and workshops are run constantly; it is, however, extremely difficult to overcome entrenched values and attitudes, and the likelihood is that changes will be generational in timescale.

WOMEN IN MANAGEMENT

As we have seen, the status of women in Botswana has changed dramatically over the last five decades. Once the underdogs, virtually chattels, and practically owned, with very few rights compared to men, women are now increasingly independent and making a very significant contribution to public and private life. Today, women play a high-profile role in

Dorcas Makgato-Malesu, former Minister of Trade and Industry, in 2012.

the management of the country's economy, both in government and in the private sector. To its great credit the government has sought to improve the level of gender equality, and there are several women in responsible and senior positions. In all sectors women are being recognized and, while the target of absolute equality may not yet have been reached, progress toward that goal is very good. There are many women, young and old, who are extremely impressive, and it is encouraging that among the younger generation, especially those with a good education and some years of work experience gained outside the country, there is the promise of many more to come.

As a very general comment, it may be true to say that, perhaps because of their past, women today are seen by many as hardworking, reliable, consistent, trustworthy, and preferable to men for many positions.

PRESENTATION AND LISTENING STYLES

The general quality of business presentations in Botswana is not very sophisticated. The flip chart and overhead projector are definitely on the way out, and are being replaced by poorly conducted Microsoft PowerPoint presentations, upon which reliance is sadly excessive.

A general failure to appreciate the value and nuances of individual presentations, together with a lack of confidence in even considering undertaking such a thing, often leads to situations where the speaker will put up a slide and then carefully, word for word, read aloud to his audience exactly what they can read for themselves.

Interestingly, the Batswana are extremely good listeners, and pay close attention to the spoken word. The conventional markers indicating attentive listening also apply in Botswana: eye contact, body language, questions, and so on.

NEGOTIATIONS

The negotiation style is essentially Western, and there are only one or two things to note. It is more important than usual to ensure that one is speaking with decision makers, as opposed to those many individuals in the management line who would like to be considered as decision makers, but who, in fact, have no such authority. In a business community that has a fairly centralized decision-making ethos, it is important to get as close as possible to the actual decision maker.

Another very African approach in a negotiating situation is not to state an opening price or position but rather to ask what a potential buyer is prepared to offer. This always starts the buyer off on the wrong foot, because, if he does make an offer, it tells the seller what he is prepared to pay and leaves the field open for the seller to negotiate the price upward. One has to be prepared to counter this strategy by insisting on some indication of price from the seller or by offering a very low price in the first instance.

CONTRACTS

The common law on contract has its roots in Roman–Dutch law and is standard across southern Africa: the law can be and is enforced. The strength of a contract depends very much on the level of business at which it is made. Contracts associated with major infrastructure projects, for example, are written to international standards and are respected, and, if necessary, able to be enforced. Having said that, however, does not mean that all contracts are respected.

It is, for example, customary to rent a house on a lease, say for a year or two years, but tenants will routinely break the lease, often without notifying the landlord. While the lease certainly could be enforced through the legal system, one can be certain that it will take a very long time, the process will be costly, and the defendant, at the end of it all, will have prepared himself well to show that he has no means. In these circumstances it may be better not to bother.

Shopkeepers are generally good at replacing items that turn out to be damaged or faulty, but returning something because one has changed one's mind would require considerable powers of persuasion!

PLANNING

At government level, planning for the country at large is routinely and successfully carried out with regular five-year national development plans. Similar planning processes permeate the infrastructure of local government and, looking at the success of the country as a whole, one is easily persuaded that planning is effectively done. At that level, so it appears to be. It is at the micro level that performance is not as good. Much planning is marred by inexperience, both of what is being planned for and the appropriate quality standards associated with it. Naturally there is resentment at having to use expatriate expertise and a strong desire to have a task done locally. Poor supervision (see above) also tends to exacerbate shortcomings in planning.

TEAMWORK AND MANAGEMENT

In common with management philosophy across the world there is, in Botswana, increasing emphasis on the idea of teams and teamwork. It is a philosophy well suited to the Batswana, who traditionally favored unanimity, cohesion, and a lack of dissension as important survival strategies. That said, teams need more than agreement and togetherness. Taking personal responsibility for one's work and motivation are new and somewhat threatening ideas for many. It is widely believed that the "boss" is almost wholly responsible for an individual's motivation, and there is often resistance to the idea that the individual himself has any control over or responsibility for it.

There is an obstacle in professional management in Botswana that visitors need to be aware of. They may come from a country with a "driven" work ethic, where productivity levels are honed to a high level of effectiveness, and where they have been accustomed to setting clear goals and getting unequivocal results on time, on target, as expected. This is not likely to be their Botswana experience.

Although the aims will be the same, the methods by which they will be achieved will be different, and the quality of the staff working on the project will also be different. This will almost certainly produce a result somewhat less than expected or, if the expected results are obtained, at the cost of much greater management input, effort, and time.

TAKING THE INITIATIVE

If there is a constant call that rings through the corridors of Botswana's commercial world it is, "Why can't I find people who will take the initiative?" The call accurately reflects the current situation: it is difficult to find people who will use their initiative. Traditionally for the Batswana, consensus, agreement, cohesion have all been vital elements. To stand out, to be different from the group, is to risk becoming a "tall poppy," to risk being seen as different, as putting yourself above others as smarter or cleverer, and to risk, as a result, the resentment and antagonism of your peers.

It is also true that the scope for individuals in a relatively uneducated and inexperienced workforce to act on their own initiative is often strictly limited, and so it is difficult for people to find the opportunity to use their initiative. It is such experiences that give rise to calls from the workforce for "Empowerment," "Participation," and "Consultation." Of course, there are many Batswana who are extremely competent and it therefore behoves the foreign manager to study his staff carefully and delegate with care, perhaps allowing small but incremental opportunities for individual growth.

DECISION MAKING

The Batswana are not known for their speed in decision making, especially at government level, where procrastination is common. However, it is a characteristic that, when a negative decision is made, it will not be reversed. It is considered extremely bad form to say "no" and then change your mind.

It is also true that, because of the nature and educational level of the general working population, the level at which decisions are made in an organization is surprisingly high. The tendency toward centralization is thus quite marked, even for very simple decisions and questions. For this reason it is always good practice to test first whether the person you are speaking to has the authority to make the decision you require rather than to rely on your assumption that that is the case. Failure to do so will result in your repeating your request to three or four different people before getting to the one person who can give an answer.

STARTING A BUSINESS IN BOTSWANA

For some decades after independence economic growth in Botswana was led by government, which set about using its immense wealth to develop the economy. This produced years of extraordinary growth as offices, roads, railways, airports, schools, and all the apparatus of a modern state were gradually put in place. To a large extent that has now been achieved and so, for this and other reasons, government spending has fallen.

Growth, however, is still needed to absorb the never-ending stream of graduates from secondary schools and the country's university, and so it is that huge government resources are now available to stimulate non-governmental, entrepreneurial, economic growth. There are a number of government agencies that aim at attracting foreign investment and facilitating the establishment of foreign businesses in Botswana. At the same time there are many incentives for citizens to take entrepreneurial initiatives and start developing their own enterprises.

Although it has been said before in this book, it is always important to remember how far Botswana has come in the last fifty-five years. The country has been on an incredibly steep learning curve, has achieved great things, and its people are still desperately keen to learn and to go on improving. It is largely these facts that make foreigners want to come back time and time again and, in many cases, to settle here.

CHAPTER NINE

COMMUNICATING

LANGUAGE

English

The two official languages of the country are Setswana and English, and the latter is widely spoken throughout the country, especially in the towns and in tourist destinations. In rural areas English is much less common and, indeed, to find an English speaker in a village is often difficult. However, in the towns and cities, such people as hotel staff, government officials, garage attendants, waitresses, and shop assistants will all be able to communicate sufficiently. English is very much the language of commerce.

It is, nevertheless, important for visitors to realize that unfamiliar accents sometimes make it very difficult for the Batswana to understand them. They should also be aware of the dangers inherent in asking direct questions that require a "yes" or "no" answer. People like to help and to be positive, and you may be given the answer it is thought you are seeking rather than the answer you need!

Setswana

Many report that Setswana is quite a difficult language to learn. Acquiring the skill is made more difficult because so many Batswana in the towns speak good English. Nevertheless, there are certain everyday words and phrases that are easy to acquire, and go a long way to convince local people that one does respect their language and is making an effort to learn it:

"*Dumela*" is a universal greeting for all times of day or night. Add "*rra*," if you are greeting a man, or "*mma*" for a woman. One can add the word "*Legae*," meaning, "How are you?" to which the standard response is "*Keteng*," "All is well."
Kealeboga: "Thank you."
Ketumetse: "I am happy/contented."
Gosiame: "This is fine, it's all OK." (Note that the "G" is soft and pronounced as "Ho.")

Locals really appreciate the use by foreigners of even a few words of their language, and the effort to acquire them is more than justified by the results.

Foreign Languages

The use of foreign languages is not widespread in Botswana. Within tiny expatriate communities they might be used but, beyond that, the vast majority of the population speak Setswana as a lingua franca. Bantu languages other than Setswana will be spoken in the districts that form the heartland of a particular language group, for example, Sekalanga being the language of the Kalanga people in the north of the country.

VOICES LOUDER THAN WORDS

Visitors may well notice that when two or more Batswana walk down a road or past a house and are talking to each other, they may be doing so in very loud voices. This is a common experience of foreigners in Africa, and the generally accepted explanations have their roots deep in the traditional past: people speak loudly in order to warn wild animals of their approach; or people speak loudly so that there can be no suspicion that they are plotting or planning mischief—by speaking loudly they obviously have nothing to hide!

Libraries

In an effort to encourage literacy the government maintains libraries in all large towns. A great deal of money is spent on these resources and they are well stocked; borrowing is possible. Mobile libraries visit the larger villages.

BODY LANGUAGE

Perhaps the most striking observation that visitors will make is how younger women, especially in the rural areas and among those with little education, cast down their eyes and deliberately avoid making eye contact. This is not rudeness: it is customary behavior that is required from young women, particularly when they are dealing with strangers. Of course, with young city folk this happens less and less.

It is very common to see men holding hands, and should a male visitor who is on friendly terms with a local man meet him, he may find that, after greeting, they will be walking side by side with hands held for a few steps. The initial encounter itself is very Western in style, and might start with a handshake. This comes in two forms: the conventional Western style of hand-gripping-hand, or gripping hands, gripping thumbs, and then gripping hands again. If two men know each other well and have not seen each other for some time it is normal, while clasping hands conventionally, to touch right shoulder to right shoulder and embrace lightly. Increasingly among the more sophisticated, it is becoming common for a man who is meeting a woman he knows well to kiss her lightly on one or both cheeks.

Generally speaking, the Batswana are less conscious of physical closeness than some foreigners and may often stand closer to you than you find comfortable.

THE MEDIA

The Press
The government produces a daily newspaper, entitled the *Daily News*, which is available free throughout the country provided it is collected from various distribution points. It is published in English but has a section in Setswana and covers both national and international news.

There are several privately owned newspapers, the number of which varies from four or five to six or seven. These tend to be locally distributed and are available for purchase. All are published weekly, and depend on advertising to supplement their sales revenue.

Ostensibly and legally, the press is free, but to what extent this is really true is hard to say. The press is sometimes critical of the government, yet it is only a few years ago that the government, expressing dissatisfaction with the contents of a particular newspaper, threatened to withdraw all government advertising from it. As the government completely dominates the economy—and so small is the private sector by comparison—this threat, had it been carried out, would probably have brought about the ruin of the publication.

Radio and TV

The government operates two radio stations, RB 1 and RB 2, which reach the whole country and are broadcast

Presenter at ICE100, Botswana's pioneering Internet radio station.

on both FM and medium wave. The former is almost completely in Setswana, while the latter is aimed at a more general audience, has advertising, and broadcasts fairly equally in both official languages.

In Gaborone, the capital city, there are two private stations: "Gabs" FM, aimed at a general audience, and "Yarona," aimed very much at the younger generation. Both are mostly in English, run advertising, and operate on licenses issued by the government.

The government recently spent a great deal of money building what is said to be a "state of the art" TV broadcasting station in Gaborone, but the country currently lacks the skilled professional staff to take full advantage of it. There is only one channel broadcasting over the whole country, via satellite, with limited local content. Aside from the decoder and dish the service is free, just as it is locally in Gaborone via an ordinary antenna. BBC World is transmitted in the morning for three hours and a number of foreign "soaps" are broadcast in the evening. Efforts are being made to broadcast more locally produced programs.

SERVICES

Telephone
Botswana's telephone system is world-class, although there are occasional glitches on some lines when the

rains start; these are quickly repaired and the system runs well. Although prices are falling, telephone calls are expensive when compared to European prices, for example.

Although there are approximately 100,000 telephone lines, what amazes people in this country is that, despite the small population of some 2.3 million people, there were a staggering 3,353,000 registered sim cards in circulation in March 2019. When the service began in the 1990s, many doubted that one single provider would survive, never mind the two to whom licenses were granted. In 2020 there were three independent service providers. Certainly nobody believed that cell phones would become as widespread as they are today. It would be a mistake, though, to think that such a number is indicative of prosperity: the great majority run on the "pay-as-you-go" method, and the Batswana are past masters at "SMSing" (known as "short message service" in southern Africa, and text messaging elsewhere) and getting others to phone them and bear the cost of the call!

Be cautioned that, while cell phone coverage is quite good, existing in all cities and major towns including most large villages, there are significant gaps between these places. At a guess about 80 percent of the country does not have coverage (mostly because there are no, or only a few, people living there), and most certainly wilderness areas are without it. With the exception of those parts of Chobe Game Reserve close to Kasane, the areas of Savute, Moremi Game Reserve, and most of the Okavango have no coverage at all.

Electricity Supply

Botswana has two, soon to be three, coal-fired power plants that feed into the national 220-volt grid. There are currently some performance issues and demand has grown at such a rapid rate that the country is not meeting its own needs. A significant percentage of Botswana's electrical power is now purchased from South Africa—a somewhat invidious position as that country itself is rapidly growing short of power and may soon not be able to meet Botswana's demands. Extensions of the existing power plant are in hand but have not yet been completed. It is possible that power shortages may be anticipated.

Internet

There are a number of independent e-mail and Internet service providers, and connection is possible through ADSL lines and by wireless. Speeds are typically in the order of 4Mbs, perfectly adequate for domestic use. For big corporate businesses and other large-scale users, Metrointernet, facilitated by Botswana Telecommunications Corporation (BTC), is available on leased lines with speeds of up to 100Mbs.

The country relies on a number of international connections, including those through South Africa, Namibia, via the West African Coastal Service (WACS), and the EASSY connection via the East African coast. Fast and reliable Internet connections are available in all major centers but rural connectivity is more problematic.

In Botswana the Internet rules! With so many smartphones, almost all have access, although the use is somewhat limited due to levels of wealth and the relatively high cost of data. The sharing of music, photographs, selfies, and Google searches is now as common in Botswana as it is anywhere else on earth.

THE IMPACT OF THE NEW TECHNOLOGIES

Much of the fascination of Botswana is the experience of living in such a rapidly changing society. The generational gaps are significant and especially noticeable because of the compressed time spans within which they have taken place. Whereas change in, say, Europe might have taken place over centuries, in Africa it happens in decades, and sometimes even just years.

Changes are more dramatic and happen more rapidly, and nowhere in Botswana is this more obvious and dramatic than in the impact of the cell phone and social media.

Cell phones are now ubiquitous. With a national population a little in excess of 2.2 million people, there are more than 3.3 million registered sim cards and almost every individual has basic cell phone literacy. The number of smartphones is rather harder to estimate but their use is very widespread. As a consequence, the use of social media is widespread and growing: Twitter, Facebook, Google, various dating apps, and WhatsApp are daily terms and widely used commercially and by government.

In common with many countries, Botswana is the victim of an ever-growing gap between rich and poor, with disposable income significantly influencing one's choice of phone and hence one's apparent social ranking. For this reason, older (inherently more conservative) people tend not to dominate the smartphone market, while the younger generations and the commercial world most definitely do. In effect, the modern phone has become a marker of social differentiation.

With excellent global connectivity through the Internet, every kind of content is available to many at the touch of a finger and there is a rapidly developing "Westernization" of the population, particularly the younger generation who own the right phones, which are therefore proving to be an extraordinarily effective catalyst for social change.

Take Christmas as an example. In former times at the festive season men and women working in the towns and cities would return by bus and car to their home villages where a large and traditional family get-together would take place, accompanied by much singing, dancing, and perhaps the slaughter of a cow or goat. To the chagrin of the older population, this is much less common today, especially among younger people.

Western values and norms pour in through the Internet and via the phones and television, influencing younger people in the cities, who now choose not to take the long uncomfortable journey home, preferring to party, watch movies, or simply hang out with their peers.

Another interesting example is standing in line. Following the dictates of the traditional Botswana philosophy of *Botho* (meaning universal caring, politeness, and mutual respect by people for each other) a recent president declared that older, retired people should be ushered to the front of any line in shops, banks, government offices, and the like. Such an order was entirely within the expectations of the more conservative part of the population, and for quite a long time the practice was followed, but with the departure of the president it has fallen away again. The fact is that traditional respect for the elderly by the youth is diminishing. So too is the traditional greeting ritual, under attack as youngsters turn to Western jargon instead of the more formal enquiries about how you are, how you slept, and how the family is.

At dizzying speeds, smartphones have been catapulted into life in Botswana with new apps appearing every day, almost. New technology is everywhere. Once it was messages and talking; now it's online banking, payment of water and electricity bills, online shopping, watching movies, setting up dates. Even credit cards are following the trend with a "swipe" ("swish" in some European countries) facility on most. It is true to say now that in Botswana media use and functionality is no different from other parts of the world.

Mail

Botswana Postal Services operate an efficient service, both locally and worldwide. They also have a courier system that works well regionally, and they offer an Expedited Mail Service (EMS) delivering small packages throughout the world directly to the addressee. There are also several private courier companies.

CONCLUSION

Botswana is, in many ways, the gem of southern Africa. Its immense diamond wealth has made it possible to achieve great things, but it has been its conservative values, strongly held, that have provided the springboard for its younger generations to leap into the modern world. With such a start the country has avoided the corruption that has so blighted other potentially wealthy African states. There is no tribal conflict, there is no widespread corruption, and modern democratic institutions flourish in a country with deeply rooted traditions of consultation and participation.

In this book we have looked at the way Botswana's past continues to influence the present. We have seen a country in transition, effecting a change within a few decades that other countries have taken centuries to achieve. Conservative and cautious the government may be, but in a continent beset by troubles it is a rewarding experience to be among the people of a small nation that is managing the transition from the past to the future, from poverty to wealth, with such commitment and success. The Batswana are determined to hold on to what they have and to build a nation that will be an example to the rest of Africa and to the world. You cannot visit Botswana without being touched by the magic of the place and the warmth and friendliness of the people, their love of laughter, and their inherent respect for others.

APPENDIX: GLOSSARY

Basarwa: the plural form of the word *Sarwa*, meaning a single Bushman.

Bakhalagari: descendants of early occupiers of Botswana. Bantu but not Tswana in origin.

Bogadi (or **Lobola**): bride wealth—the "price" paid for a wife.

Cattle post: a location in the bush with a borehole and where a man's cattle will be based.

CBNRM: Community Based Natural Resource Management.

Chibuku: a traditional beer made from maize.

Dikgosi: plural of *kgosi*, chiefs.

DWNP: Department of Wildlife and National Parks.

Great Trek: the mass exodus of Boer farmers by ox-wagon out of the Cape into the African hinterland that took place in 1834–5.

Kalahari: from historical times a so-called desert but, strictly, a semiarid region characterized by very low and erratic annual rainfall. In geological times it was a true desert, traces of which can be identified today by vast areas of wind-blown sand and relic sand dunes, all now clothed in sparse grass and shrubs. At its greatest reach, in the Cretaceous Period, this ancient desert extended from the Orange River in South Africa, engulfing some 75 percent of Botswana's western land area to beyond the Congo River, and even today it forms the most extensive continuous area of sand in the world.

Kgosi (pl. **Dikgosi**): a tribal chief.

Kgotla: traditional meeting place in every Tswana village where the chief or headman deals with tribal matters. Originally confined to men only, now open to both sexes.

Khadi: a traditional alcoholic beverage.

Khama III: Ruled as chief of the Ngwato people, 1872–3 and 1874–1923. A powerful and successful chief who accepted Christianity, banned alcohol, and steered his tribe through much of the tumultuous nineteenth century.

Lobola: see *Bogadi.*

Lolwapa: a low wall surrounding the courtyard in front of a traditional dwelling.

Mokoro: a wooden, dugout canoe (pl. *mekoro*).

Mzilikazi: Chief of the Matabele people who raided eastern Botswana in the 1830s and eventually established themselves in the southern part of modern Zimbabwe in the town now called Bulawayo.

NGO: Nongovernmental Organization.

Pan: a wind formed surface feature of semiarid zones. Usually hard clay, semicircular, usually bare of vegetation (although occasionally covered with a coarse grass), collecting rainwater and holding it for a few months.

San: also known as Bushmen—autochthonous inhabitants of southern Africa.

Seswaa: a traditional Tswana meat dish consisting of boiled meat beaten into a fibrous state and eaten with green vegetables.

FURTHER READING

Bailey, Adrian, and Robyn Keene-Young. *Okavango, a Journey*. Cape Town: Struik Publishers, 2006.

Campbell, Alec. *The Guide to Botswana*. Johannesburg: Winchester Press, 1980.

Campbell, Alec, and Mike Main. *Guide to Greater Gaborone*. Gaborone: M. Main, 2003.

Campbell, Alec, and Thomas Tlou. *History of Botswana*. Gaborone: Macmillan Botswana, 1984.

Denbow, James, and Phenyo C. Thebe. *Culture and Customs of Botswana*. Westport: Greenwood Press, 2006.

Dutfield, Michael. *A Marriage of Inconvenience: The Persecution of Seretse and Ruth Khama*. London: Unwin Hyman, 1990.

Johnson, Peter, Anthony Bannister, and Alf Wanneburgh. *The Bushmen*. Cape Town: Struik Publishers, 1979.

Lee, Richard. *The !Kung San: Men, Women and Work in a Foraging Society*. Cambridge: Cambridge University Press, 1979.

Main, Mike. *Kalahari: Life's Variety in Dune and Delta*. Johannesburg: Southern Book Publishers, 1987.

Main, Mike. *African Adventurer's Guide to Botswana*. Cape Town: Struik Publishers, 2002.

Mendelsohn, John, and Selma el Obeid. *Okavango River, the Flow of a Lifeline*. Cape Town: Struik Publishers, 2004.

Schapera, Isaac, and John L. Comaroff (rev. ed.). *The Tswana*. London, New York: Kegan Paul International in association with the International African Institute, 1991.

Tobias, Phillip (ed.). *The Bushmen: San Hunters and Herders of Southern Africa*. Cape Town: Human and Rousseau Publishers, 1978.

The Botswana Society publishes an annual semi-academic journal called *Botswana Notes and Records*. It contains articles on virtually every realm of study in the country. The Society also has publications on the various symposia and workshops it holds. All are available from the Botswana Society Offices:

P.O. Box 71 Gaborone. Tel.: +267 3919673. E-mail: botsoc@info.bw.

The University of Botswana's "Botswana Room" and the National Library Service have extensive collections of publications on Botswana; both are open to the public.

PICTURE CREDITS

Cover image: *Quiver trees, so called because of the traditional San practice of hollowing out their branches to form quivers for their arrows.* © Canva by 2630ben.

Shutterstock.com: pages 12, 17, 46, 48, 58, 61, 62, 73, 96, 101, 114, 178 by Lucian Coman; 18 by Dietmar Temps; 34, 39, 121 by Roger Brown Photography; 91 by Dewald Kirsten; 98 by Claudiovidri; 122 by Srijit Bhaumick; 135 by Petr Bonek; 136 by 2639ben; 142 by Fedor Selivanov; 146 by Art Konovalov.

Unsplash: pages 14 by Wynand Uys; 88 by Mohau Mannathoko.

Pixabay.com: pages 118 by tshekisoboman.

Flickr: pages 66 by GovernmentZA; 117, 186 WycliffeSA, photo by Zeke duPlessis; 137 by Vaughn McShane.

Z.A. Pinterest.com: pages 36–7.

Botswana Tourism Organization: page 103 by Zoran Nikolic.

Images on these pages reproduced under Creative Commons Attribution-Share Alike 4.0 International license: page 30 © Ophir Mizrah; 68, 123, 129 © Mompati Dikunwane; 78 © Peter Grobbee; 113 © Mahyars; 119 © SanDanceVR; 133 © Bernard Gagnon; 134 © AoneMokwena; 139 © Jedesto; 148 © ThusoMotlasuping; 158 HenryNewman12; 184 © Jessletshwiti.

Creative Commons Attribution-Share Alike 3.0 Unported license: pages 7© TUBS

Creative Commons Attribution-Share Alike 2.0 Generic license: pages 42 © Jorge Láscar from Australia; 44 © Martijn.Munneke from Netherlands; 138 © Kevin Pluck; 169 © UNCTAD.

Creative Commons Attribution-Share Alike license: page 164 © Ministry of Micro, Small & Medium Enterprises (GODL-India).

INDEX